ALSO BY GORE VIDAL

NOVELS

Williwaw
In a Yellow Wood
The City and the Pillar
The Season of Comfort
A Search for the King
Dark Green, Bright Red
The Judgment of Paris
Messiah
Julian
Washington D.C.
Myra Breckinridge
Two Sisters
Burr
Myron
1876
Kalki
Creation
Duluth
Lincoln
Myra Breckinridge and Myron
Empire
Hollywood
Live from Golgotha
The Smithsonian Institution
The Golden Age

SHORT STORIES

A Thirsty Evil

PLAYS

An Evening with Richard Nixon
Weekend
Romulus
The Best Man
Visit to a Small Planet

ESSAYS

Rocking the Boat
Reflections Upon a Sinking Ship
Homage to Daniel Shays
Matters of Fact and Fiction
The Second American Revolution
At Home
Screening History
United States
The Last Empire

MEMOIR

Palimpsest

HISTORY

Inventing a Nation: Washington, Adams, Jefferson

PAMPHLETS

The Decline and Fall of the American Empire (1992)
The American Presidency (1998)
Perpetual War for Perpetual Peace (2002)
Dreaming War (2003)

GORE VIDAL

IMPERIAL AMERICA

Reflections on the United States of Amnesia

NATION
BOOKS

IMPERIAL AMERICA: *Reflections on the United States of Amnesia*

Published by
Nation Books
An Imprint of Avalon Publishing Group
245 West 17th St., 11th Floor
New York, NY 10011

AVALON
publishing group incorporated

Nation Books is a co-publishing venture of the Nation Institute and
Avalon Publishing Group Incorporated.

Library Cataloging-in-Publication Data is available.

ISBN 1-56025-744-X

9 8 7 6 5 4 3

Design by Simon M. Sullivan
Printed in the United States of America
Distributed by Publishers Group West

CONTENTS

NOTE

I dedicated my last political "pamphlet," *Dreaming War,* to Publius, the joint authors of *The Federalist.* Unfortunately, since now continues to be the time for all good men and women to come to the aid of their country, I invoke, once more, the ghosts of Madison, Hamilton and John Jay—may we prevail.

—GORE VIDAL
March 22, 2004

INTRODUCTION TO
THE 2005 EDITION

The four most beautiful words in the English language are "I told you so." For several years I have been writing and saying in books, pamphlets, and even, occasionally, inside the electronic zoo currently inhabited by a single rabid Fox that there was no proof that Saddam Hussein had weapons of mass destruction nor was he the slightest threat to the United States or even to "our" oil fields which are, by divine right, American property despite the deity's characteristic misjudgment in placing them on land that belongs to Moslems who are fellow children of the Good Book just like us Christians and Jews located all over the lot. Why the deity misplaced those specific oil and natural gas fields probably has more to do with a busy workload than any desire to make mischief for the residents of the U.S., the nation that produced Henry Ford. Plainly, the deity had far too much work keeping the poor Florida lady linked to her lifeline as well as the smitten pope in Heaven's anteroom, not to mention all those hurtling souls like reverse comets from the Middle East. I suspect a weary, fed up deity might, in a moment of weakness, just conjure up another tsunami or two to get rid of us once and for all.

Meanwhile, I have been reading a confirmation of what I have been denounced for saying since 9/11: "Spy Agencies Called 'Dead Wrong' in Prewar Analyses on Iraq." This story in the *Los Angeles Times* is billed as "Text of Letter to President Bush." The letter is from the Commission on the Intelligence Capabilities of the United States regarding weapons of mass destruction. These "disinterested" experts conclude that the "intelligence community was dead wrong in almost all of its prewar judgments about Iraq's weapons of mass destruction." So far so good. So true. Now, alas, watch the buck not so subtly pass: "What the intelligence professionals told you about Saddam Hussein's program was what they believed. They were wrong." Thus, the Commission shifts responsibility to the professional intelligence gatherers while carefully protecting the president and vice president who were gung ho for an invasion of Iraq *before* 9/11. After 9/11, all intelligence was carefully bent to show what horrible dangers we faced from the monolithic Taliban and their associates Al-Qaida, joint-master of every sort of nuclear and biological weapon ready, in a mere forty-five minutes, to destroy us because we are good and they are evil according to the best information of the oil and gas junta that governs us. Certainly if they were not eager to remove us from the planet before we wrecked Afghanistan and Iraq, two countries that had done us no harm, they are probably now more than ever ready to bring on their suicide planes in order to level our alabaster cities.

I am sometimes asked how I was so certain that Saddam and company lacked the horrendous weapons our rulers insisted they had. Am I some sort of secret agent? No. But I do live in Europe part of the year where every reader of the serious press knows exactly how our governing junta is constantly cooking up "evidence" through our various intelligence agencies in order to excite the media to terrify us into wars of preemptive aggression against nations with enormous oil reserves, nations plainly guided by Satan who is being transformed by our dizzy media into a Moslem or, at the very least, prophet.

In the year since the first publication of *Imperial America,* my warnings about how the electronic voting machines could be so easily rigged during the '04 election certainly came true in Ohio as Representative John Conyers demonstrates in "Preserving Democracy: What Went Wrong in Ohio: Status Report of the House Judiciary Committee Democratic Staff, January 5, 2005," soon to be, I assume, invisibly published as are those documents that are critical of the way that corporate America arranges elections for us while their media covers up those crimes, great and small, that are committed in the process. Although many Ohioans were aware that games were being played by those supervising the election of November '04, none of those accountable, like their secretary of state, has thus far answered the questions put to them by Congressman Conyers. Also, the companies that make the electronic machines from Diebold to Triad are owned by die-hard Republicans who insist that because of "trade secrets" only their employees can examine the machines. Thus, our elections our privatized.

Although poll taking is something of a craze in this least democratic period of our history, nothing much seems to penetrate the polled. Although they are standing firmly against the presidential efforts to replace Social Security (in no more imminent danger of collapse than Saddam Hussein possessed weapons of mass destruction pre-invasion) with an "investment bonanza" for Wall Street, there seems to be no very active political inquiry against what is intended to be the greatest gold rush since the Klondike. So much that once provoked national outrage seems nowadays to fade away like a TV commercial. One thinks of the horrors of the prison system that the military has been running from Cuba to Iraq and who knows where else? Those in charge, starting with the president, secretary of defense, and so on down the line of command, are automatically exempted from all accountability. A few enlisted men and women have been charged and it is reasonable to assume that the killings and torture will continue as usual, if not on an even larger scale. Certainly, we shall not be informed. But to the extent that the odd brave journalist-publisher who goes public with information about our military prisons, a bizarre reflection of what goes on at home, will be drowned out by three-minute TV rebuttals and denials in the mainstream print media.

Question: is it that we really don't know these things? Or that we know or suspect quite a bit but are fearful of seeming to be out of step with a vast propaganda machine? Or, finally, has some traditional American spirit—ever skeptical of authority—been switched off for lack of fuel?

This is all deeply puzzling, profoundly un-American. Sooner or later in our history, injustices, if permitted to go on too long, have suffered from a sort of spontaneous combustion as in 1860 when the institution of slavery became so incandescent that civil war broke out. There are similar omens and portents today that we are approaching a great crisis in our affairs when a hugely wealthy minority has set itself in opposition to a more marginalized, even disenfranchised, majority that already shows signs of awakening to the danger to us all. When it does, no corporate conglomerate will be strong enough to protect the tyrants.

—Gore Vidal
Los Angeles
April 2005

I

ONE

STATE OF THE UNION: 2004

I

In the sixties and seventies of the last unlamented century, there was a New York television producer named David Susskind. He was commercially successful; he

was also, surprisingly, a man of strong political views which he knew how to present so tactfully that networks were often unaware of just what he was getting away with on their—our—air. Politically, he liked to get strong-minded guests to sit with him at a round table in a ratty building at the corner of Broadway and 42nd Street. Sooner or later, just about everyone of interest appeared on his program. Needless to say, he also had time for Vivien Leigh to discuss her recent divorce from Laurence Olivier, which summoned forth the mysterious cry from the former Scarlett O'Hara, "I am deeply sorry for any woman who was not married to Larry Olivier." Since this took in several billion ladies (not to mention those gentlemen who might have offered to fill, as it were, the breach), Leigh caused a proper stir, as did the ballerina Alicia Markova, who gently assured us that "a Markova comes only once every hundred years or so."

I suspect it was the dim lighting on the set that invited such naked truths. David watched his pennies. I don't recall how, or when, we began our "States of the Union" programs. But we did them year after year. I would follow whoever happened to be president, and I'd correct his "real" state of the union with one of my own, improvising from questions that David would prepare. I was a political pundit because in a 1960 race for the House of Representatives (upstate New York), I got more votes than the head of the ticket, JFK; in 1962, I turned down the Democratic nomination for U.S. Senate on the sensible ground that it was not winnable; I also had a pretty good memory in those days, now a-jangle with warning bells as I try to recall the national deficit or, more poignantly, where I last saw my glasses.

I've just come across my "State of the Union" as of 1972. Apparently, I gave it fifteen times across the country, ending with Susskind's program. Questions and answers from the audience were the most interesting part of these excursions. As I look back over the texts of what we talked about, I'm surprised at how to the point we often were on subjects seldom mentioned in freedom's land, today.

In 1972, I begin: "According to the polls, our second principal concern today is the breakdown of law and order." (What, I wonder, was the first? Let's hope it was the pointless, seven-year—at that point—war in Southeast Asia). I noted that to die-hard conservatives "law and order" is usually a code phrase meaning "get the blacks." To what anorexic, vacant-eyed blond women on TV refer as the "liberal elite," the careful—that is, slow—elimination of poverty was what we were pushing. Anything more substantive would be regarded as "communism," put forward by dupes. But then, I say very mildly, we have only one political party in the U.S., the Property Party, with two right wings, Republican and Democrat. Since I tended to speak to conservative audiences in such civilized places as Medford, Oregon; Parkersburg, West Virginia; Longview, Washington, there are, predictably, a few gasps at this rejection of so much received opinion. There are also quite a few nods from interested citizens who find it difficult at election time to tell the parties apart. Inspired, by the nods, I start to geld the lily, as the late Sam Goldwyn used to say. Republicans are often stupider and more doctrinaire than the Democrats, who are cuter, a bit more corrupt (sigh of relief) but willing to make small—very small—adjustments when the poor, the black, the anti-imperialists (Curious—I was already characterizing our crazed adventure in Vietnam as imperial, instead of yet another proof of our irrepressible, invincible altruism, ever eager to bring light to those who dwell in darkness.)

I should note that in the thirty-one years since this particular state of the union, our political vocabulary has been turned upside down. Although the secret core to each presidential election is who can express his hatred of the African-Americans most subtly (to which today can be added Latinos and "elite liberals"—a fantasy category associated with working film actors who have won Academy Awards)—and, of course, this season the so-called marriage-minded gays. So-called because there is no such human or mammal category (sex is a continuum) except in the great hollow pumpkin head of that gambling dude who has anointed himself the nation's moralist-in-chief, William "Bell Fruit" Bennett.

Back to the time machine. In some ways, looking at past states of the union, it is remarkable how things tend to stay the same. Race-gender wars are always on our overcrowded back burners. There is also—always—a horrendous foreign enemy at hand ready to blow us up in the night out of hatred for our Goodness and rosy plumpness. In 1972, when I started my tour at the Yale Political Union, the audience was packed with hot-eyed Neocons-to-be, though the phrase was not yet in use, as the inventors of Neo-conery were still Trotskyites to a man or woman or even "Bell Fruit," trying to make it in New York publishing.

I also stay away from the failing economy. "I leave it to my friend, Ken Galbraith, the solving of the current depression." If they appear to know who Galbraith is, I remark how curious that his fame should be based on two books, *The Liberal Hour*, published just as the right-wing Nixon criminals were trying to highjack the election of 1972 (the Watergate was bursting open when I began my tour), and *The Affluent Society*, published shortly before we had a cash-flow problem.

In the decades since this state of the union, the United States has more people, per capita, locked away in prisons than any other country while the sick economy of '72 is long forgotten as worse problems—and deficits—beset us. For one thing, we no longer live in a nation, but in a Homeland. In 1972: "roughly 80 percent of police work in the United States has to do with the regulation of our private morals. By that I mean, controlling what we smoke, eat, put in our veins—not to mention trying to regulate with whom and how we have sex, with whom and how we gamble. As a result our police are among the most corrupt in the Western world."

I don't think this would get the same gasp today that it did back then. I point out police collusion with gamblers, drug dealers, prostitutes or, indeed, anyone whose sexual activities have been proscribed by a series of state legal codes that were—are—the scandal of what we like to call a free society. These codes are often defended because they are very old. For instance, the laws against sodomy go back fourteen hundred years to the Emperor Justinian, who felt that there should be such a law because, "as everyone knows," he declared, "sodomy is a principal cause of earthquake."

Sodomy gets the audience's attention. "Cynically, one might allow the police their kinky pleasures in busting boys and girls who attract them if they showed the slightest interest in the protection of persons and property, which is what we pay them to do." I then suggested that "we remove from the statute books all penalties that have to do with private morals—what are called 'victimless crimes.' If a man or a woman wants to be a prostitute, that is his or her affair. Certainly, it is no business of the state what we do with our bodies sexually. Obviously, laws will remain on the books for the prevention of rape and the abuse of children while the virtue of our animal friends will continue to be protected by the SPCA." Relieved laughter at this point. He can't be serious—or is he?

I speak of legalizing gambling. Bingo players nod. Then: "All drugs should be legalized and sold at cost to anyone with a doctor's prescription." Most questions, later, are about this horrific proposal. Brainwashing on the subject begins early, ensuring that a large crop of the coming generation will become drug addicts. Prohibition always has that effect as we should have learned when we prohibited alcohol from 1919 to 1933 but, happily, for the busy lunatics who rule over us, we are permanently the United States of Amnesia. We learn nothing because we remember nothing. The period of Prohibition called the "Noble Experiment" brought on the greatest breakdown of law and order that we have ever endured—until today, of course. Lesson? Do not regulate the private lives of people because, if you do, they will become angry and anti-social, and they will get what they want from criminals who work in perfect freedom because they know how to pay off the police.

What should be done about drug addiction? By no means a good thing. As of 1970, England was the model for us to emulate. With a population of 55 million people, they had only 1,800 heroin addicts. With our 200 million people we had nearly a half-million addicts. What were they doing right? For one thing, they turned the problem over to the doctors. Instead of treating the addict as a criminal, they required him to register with a physician who then gives him, at controlled intervals, a prescription so that he can obtain his drug. Needless to say, our society, based as it is on a passion to punish others, could not bear so sensible a solution. We promptly leaned, as they say, on the British to criminalize the sale and consumption of drugs, and now the beautiful city of Edinburgh is the most drug-infested place in Europe. Another triumph for the American way.

I start to expand. "From the Drug Enforcement Agency to the FBI, we are afflicted with all sorts of secret police, busily spying on us. The FBI, since its founding, has generally steered clear of major crime like the Mafia. In fact, much of its time and energies have been devoted to spying on those Americans whose political beliefs did not please the late J. Edgar Hoover, a man who hated Commies, blacks, and women in, more or less, that order. But then the FBI has always been a collaborating tool of reactionary politicians. The Bureau also has had a nasty talent for amusing presidents with lurid dossiers on their political enemies." Now (2004) that we have ceased to be a nation under law, but a homeland where the withered Bill of Rights, like a dead trumpet vine, clings to our pseudo-Roman columns, Homeland Security appears to be uniting our secret police into a single sort of Gestapo with dossiers on everyone to prevent us, somehow or other, from being terrorized by various implacable Second and Third World enemies. Where there is no known Al Qaeda sort of threat, we create one, as in Iraq whose leader, Saddam Hussein, had no connection with 9-11 or any other proven terrorism against the United States, making it necessary for a president to invent the lawless as well as evil (to use his Bible-based language) doctrine of preemptive war based on a sort of hunch that maybe one day some country might attack us so, meanwhile, as he and his business associates covet their oil, we go to war, leveling their cities to be rebuilt by other business associates. Thus was our perpetual cold war turned hot. But of this more later.

2

My father, uncle, and two stepbrothers graduated from the U.S. Military Academy at West Point, where I was born, in the cadet hospital. Although I was brought up by a political grandfather in Washington, D.C., I was well immersed in the West Point ethos, Duty Honor Country, as was David Eisenhower, the President's grandson whom I met years later. We exchanged notes on how difficult it was to free oneself from that world; "They never let go," I said. "It's like a family."

"No," he said, "it's a religion." Although neither of us attended the Point, each was born in the cadet hospital; each went to Exeter; each grew up listening to West Pointers' gossip about one another as well as vent their political views, usually on the Far Right. At the time of the Second War, many of them thought that we were fighting the wrong side. We should be helping Hitler destroy Communism. Later, we could take care of him.

In general, they disliked politicians, Franklin Roosevelt most of all. There was also a degree of low-key anti-Semitism while pre–World War II blacks were Ellisonian invisibles. Even so, in that great war, Duty, Honor, served the country surprisingly well. Unfortunately, some served themselves well when Truman militarized the economy, providing all sorts of lucrative civilian employment for high-ranking officers. Yet it was Eisenhower himself who warned us in 1961 of the dangers of the "military-industrial complex." Unfortunately, no one seemed eager to control military spending, particularly after the Korean War, which we notoriously failed to win even though the cry "The Russians are coming!" was daily heard throughout the land. Propaganda necessary for Truman's military buildup was never questioned . . . particularly when demagogues like Senator McCarthy were destroying careers with reckless accusations that anyone able to read the *New York Times* without moving his lips was a Communist. I touched, glancingly, on all this in Nixonian 1972, when the media, Corporate America, and the highly peculiar president were creating as much terror in the populace as they could in order to build up a war machine that they thought would prevent a recurrence of the Great Depression, which had only ended in 1940 when FDR put $8 billion into rearmament and we had full employment and prosperity for the first time in that generation.

I strike a few mildly optimistic notes. "We should have a national health service, something every civilized country in the world has. Also, improved public transport (trains!). Also, schools which do more than teach conformity. Also, a cleaning of the air, of the water, of the earth before we all die of the poisons set loose by a society based on greed." Enron, of course, is decades in the future, as are the American wars of aggression against Afghanistan and Iraq.

"In the end we may offer Richard Nixon a debt of gratitude." I'm in a generous mood. "Through Nixon's awesome ineptitude we have seen revealed the political corruption of our society." (We had, of course, seen nothing yet!)

What to do? I proposed that no candidate for any office be allowed to buy space on television or in any newspaper or other medium: "This will stop cold the present system, where presidents and congressmen are bought by corporations and even by foreign countries. To become president, you will not need thirty, forty, fifty million dollars to smear your opponents and present yourself falsely on TV commercials." Were those sums ever so tiny?

Instead, television (and the rest of the media) would be required by law to provide prime time (and space) for the various candidates.

"I would also propose a four-week election period as opposed to the current four-year marathon. Four weeks is more than enough time to present the issues. To show us the candidates in interviews, debates, *un*controlled encounters, in which we can see who the candidate really is, answering tough questions, his record up there for all to examine. This ought to get a better class into politics." As I reread this, I think of Arnold Schwarzenegger. I now add: Should the candidate happen to be a professional actor, a scene or two from Shake-speare might be required during the audition . . . I mean, the primary. Also, as a tribute to Ole Bell Fruit, who favors public executions of drug dealers, these should take place on prime time as the empire gallops into its Ben-Hur phase.

I must say, I am troubled by the way that I responded to the audience's general hatred of government. I say we are the government. But I was being sophistical when I responded to their claims that our government is our enemy with that other cliché, *you* are the government. Unconsciously, I seem to have been avoiding the message that I got from one end of the country to the other: We hate this system that we are trapped in, but we don't know who has trapped us or how. We don't even know what our cage looks like because we have never seen it from the outside. Now, thirty-one years later, audiences still want to know who will let them out of the Enron-Pentagon prison with its socialism for the rich and free enterprise for the poor. So . . . welcome to 2004.

TWO

THE PRIVATIZING OF THE
AMERICAN ELECTION

I

As we enter yet another presidential election year, let us examine George W. Bush's somewhat frenzied States of the Union, exercises in political surrealism, that are often beyond mere correction much less parody.

Like Rutherford B. Hayes in the presidential election of 1876, G.W. Bush, in 2000, lost the popular vote to his Democratic rival, who appealed to the courts of Florida, where he ultimately won the right to a recount, promptly denied him by a majority of the Supreme Court of the United States at its most gleefully partisan. But, from the beginning, Florida was doomed to be counted for Bush, whose governor had recently assembled lists of mostly black citizens falsely accused of having criminal records, thus excluding them from voting at all in a state whose ballots were still being tampered with or mislaid even as the votes were being tallied. When a lawyer for Gore complained to the Court that without a rigorous recount thousands of Floridians would be denied their chance to vote for president, the Lord of Darkness, Justice Scalia, proclaimed from the bench that *no* American citizen has a Constitutional right to vote for president. Of course, this is true. We vote for the Electoral College, which directly lifts the burden from We the People while assigning that high privilege to near-anonymous electors. Without a plurality of the popular vote and without, it would seem, carrying the Electoral College (many Florida votes were never counted at all), Bush was allowed to take office without actually winning the election.

On February 27, 2001, he pranced into the Capitol to deliver his first State of the Union. He was afire with mixed metaphors. "America today is a great nation with great challenges, but greater resources. An artist using statistics as a brush could paint two very different pictures of our country. One would have warning signs: increasing poverty . . . another picture would be full of blessings: a balanced budget, big surpluses, a military that is second to none." This powerful metaphor reminds one of Michelangelo lying on his back painting the Sistine Chapel, paint dribbling onto his face. It is also poignant to recall that Bush's predecessor had left the country with a surplus of $5.6 trillion which, as of 2004, had become a deficit of over $4 trillion.

Bits and pieces of other presidents' happy phrases are stuck like raisins in the doughy text. "America is a nation at peace, not a nation at rest. Much has been given to us, and much is expected." Thanks, Abe.

What was to be expected was foreshadowed by Bush Senior's long-playing mantra. "Cut the capital-gains tax," to which Bush Junior would introduce a breathtaking tax cut for the wealthy with the rationale that the surplus he had inherited was simply the result "of taxes that were too high . . . government is charging more than it needs. The people of America have been overcharged and, on their behalf, I am asking for a refund." Thus he made it clear that he, too, favors socialism for the rich and free enterprise for the poor.

Between the first and second States of the Union, Bush confessed, on January 29, 2002, "As we gather tonight, our nation is at war, our economy is in recession, and the civilized world faces unprecedented dangers. Yet the state of our union has never been stronger." Perhaps the greatest coup of the unelected president and his handlers was, as usual, a dubious metaphor. All on his own he has declared a war on terrorism, a nonsensical notion like a war on dandruff. To resist terrorism is the norm for any government, a response best accomplished by international police and intelligence services. So why was the inappropriate word "war" used? Because only in wartime can the executive gain maximum power over the American people by replacing the checks and balances of the Constitution with an emergency apparatus currently called "homeland security." Relying upon ad hoc bits of incoherent legislation, much of the Bill of Rights can be suspended because This Is War, which it is not: at this point, the victims of 9-11 are invariably exploited, but 9-11 was the work of religious zealots and not of a country, and there can be no actual war without a country, particularly when we are faced with criminal gangs given to suicide. To assume wartime powers without a war is something new under the American sun, requiring a blizzard of lies.

Montaigne felt that lying should be a capital offense because once the tongue grows used to telling lies there is no end to it: Worse, there can be no sensible discourse between people as their society collapses due to incomprehension. Meanwhile, ever wilder rhetoric is used for unilateral military strikes against various non-offending countries like

Afghanistan, which was included in the fantasy of the war that is no war to justify our seizure of a weak country in order to control those key pipelines bringing oil from the Caspian to the world market, simultaneously benefiting the warriors' business interests. The lies about those nonexistent weapons of mass destruction in Iraq were promptly replaced by lies about phantom hordes of terrorists preparing to overthrow the United States from bases somewhere or other in that oleaginous country. If foreign terrorists are now . . . But who will ever know? The "information" that American media dispenses at the behest of homeland security daily makes less and less sense, nor does anyone much care. This regime, in its lust for ongoing wars against much of the world, no longer feels it needs to justify anything because it is, and that's that.

2

By Bush's third State of the Union, on January 20, 2003, he was the chief purveyor of bloody fantasies of which the principal one is that he is, by self-selection "a wartime president" like the big guys Lincoln and . . . uh, all the others. He begins his Third Symphony with a whopper. "We will not deny, we will not ignore, we will not pass along our problems to other Congresses, to other presidents, and other generations." That said, he proceeds to commit future generations of Americans to a catastrophic debt or, as Paul Krugman put it in the *New York Times* (7/18/03): "Mr. Bush's officials now project an astonishing $455 billion budget deficit this year and $475 billion next year . . . unpoliticized projections show a budget deficit of at least $300 billion a year as far as the eye can see."

Other inventions from the winter of 2003: "We seek peace. We strive for peace. And sometimes the peace must be defended." This is purest George Orwell. Meanwhile, Vice President Cheney's firm, Halliburton, is grimly pursuing contracts to put up new buildings in place of the ones that his colleague, Secretary of Defense Rumsfeld, has been busy knocking down in Iraq.

Among the continual boasts of the administration is how the assault on Iraq was careful to avoid any harm to civilians. According to the *Herald* of Scotland (5/23/02), "American guns, bombs, and missiles killed more civilians in the recent war in Iraq than in any conflict since Vietnam, according to preliminary assessments carried out by the UN, international aid agencies. . . . Despite U.S. boasts that this was the fastest, most clinical campaign in military history, first snapshots of 'collateral damage' indicate that between 5,000 and 10,000 Iraqi non-combatants died in the course of the hi-tech blitzkrieg."

Detailed review of the 2003 State of the Union reveals that Bush has nearly banished truth entirely. Earlier lies that had played well obviously gave him confidence that no one who mattered would ever require him to account for his violations of the False Statement Statute. (No, I'd never heard of it either.) This statute (officially Title 18: Section 1001) provides a penalty of up to five years in prison, a fine, or both to:

> whoever, in any manner within the jurisdiction of the executive, legislative, or judicial branch of the Government of the United States, knowingly and willfully (1) falsifies, conceals, or covers up by any trick, scheme or device a material fact; (2) makes any materially false,

fictitious, or fraudulent statement or representation; or (3) makes or uses any false, fictitious, or fraudulent statement or representation; or (4) makes or uses any false writing or document knowing the same to contain any materially false, fictitious, or fraudulent statement or entry . . .

In constant and reckless violation of Title 18, Section 1001, I put the case to the members of the House of Representatives that the Constitution requires you to impeach George W. Bush so that he might be then tried by the Senate for having knowingly lied to Congress and the nation.

Some State of the Union lies told the Congress and the people that they may or may not represent:

Lie One: "The British government has learned that Saddam Hussein recently sought significant quantities of uranium from Africa." Bush's speechwriters, aware that this information was false, thought that by attributing it to British intelligence Bush would not be culpable under Section 1001. But a lie to Congress is still a lie, no matter to whom attributed. Also, under another statute, members of the White House staff that prepared his speech could be prosecuted for partaking in "a criminal conspiracy to deceive Congress."

Lie Two: Bush declared that his "tax relief is for everyone who pays income tax." The Tax Policy Center of the Urban Institute and Brookings Institution notes that 8.1 million lower- and middle-income taxpayers who pay billions of dollars a year in income taxes will receive no tax cut under the new law while the 184,000 taxpayers with incomes of over $1 million a year will receive approximately $17 billion in tax cuts in

2003 alone. There have been so many lies told about the tax cuts and who benefits that even Congress should enjoy this inquiry.

In the 2002 State of the Union, Bush vowed to "strengthen the security of air travel." A year later he told Congress that he had posted (Lie Three): "50,000 newly trained federal screeners in airports." The New York *Daily News,* the newspaper with a sense of fun, sent a number of reporters with carry-on luggage containing all sorts of deadly contraband from box cutters to pepper spray. They flew out of eleven major airports on fourteen flights with six major airlines. Not one of Bush's mythical 50,000 spotted one of them. Thus did the president preserve, protect and defend us, the people, who admittedly did not actually elect him president in the first place.

Lie Four: Bush, the nature-lover and custodian of Crawford Texas's most beautiful ranch, sat down with operatives from the lumber trade in order to stop a series of catastrophic fires. Congress got the good news: "I have sent you a Healthy Forests Initiative, to help prevent the . . . fires that devastate communities, kill wildlife, and burn away millions of acres of treasured forest."

(Applause.)

CNN reported on August 22, 2002:

Central Point, Oregon (CNN)—Generating criticism from environmentalists, President Bush Thursday announced a new initiative to allow more logging in national forests, a move that he said will curb the threat of wildfires. "We need to thin," Bush said in a speech that followed a tour of some fire-ravaged land in southwestern Oregon. "We need to make our forests healthy by using some common sense. . . .We need to understand, if you let kindling build up and there's a lightning strike, you're going to get yourself a big fire."

The "Healthy Forests" initiative calls on Congress to pass laws that would "expedite procedures for forest thinning and restoration projects" and "ensure the sustainable forest management and appropriate timber production."

According to the Sierra Club:

The Healthy Forests Initiative is President Bush's response to the past year's forest fires. The initiative is based on the false assumption that landscape-wide logging will decrease forest fires.

This premise is contradicted by the general scientific consensus, which has found that logging can increase fire risk. This disconnect between what the administration says and what science says about logging and fire reveals the administration's true goal which is to use the forest fire issue to cut the public out of the public land management decision making process and to give logging companies virtually free access to our National Forests."

A press release from the nonprofit Environmental Media Services:

Washington, D.C.—President Bush's recently proposed "Healthy Forests Initiative" came under intense criticism from a group of veteran firefighters, smokejumpers and forest experts at a press conference today, moments after the Senate completed its first round of debate on the issue.

"It is ironic," said Timothy Ingalsbee, a firefighter and director of the Oregon-based Western Fire Ecology Center, "that in this time of corporate and financial scandals, President Bush wants to completely deregulate the system. They speak with the corporate elite, but never the working people. Not one of the 17,000 firefighters out on the line was ever consulted about how to protect their communities."

"The president's plan," said Randi Spivak, executive director of the American Lands Alliance, "would basically gut environmental laws, keeping the public and the courts out of the process. It proposes to pay for this work by removing the larger, fire-resistant trees."

Spivak said the plan, to be introduced by Sens. Larry Craig (R-Idaho) and Pete Domenici (R-N.M.), is primarily the work of assistant agriculture secretary Mark Rey, previously a leading lobbyist for the timber industry and author of the "now infamous salvage logging rider" in the 1990's.

Dr. Patrick Withen, a Ph.D. sociologist and veteran smokejumper who has fought fires in every Western state in the lower 48, said "the most effective place to fight fire is in a mature forest. Yet the administration is essentially trading logging [of the largest, most commercially viable trees] for thinning. This is just increasing the fire danger."

From a statement by Amy Mall, Natural Resources Defense Council Forest Policy Specialist:

Washington D.C. (August 22, 2002)—"Protecting homes and communities should be the first priority of any national forest fire plan. Unfortunately the plan unveiled today by President Bush is a smokescreen that misses the target in reducing this threat. Instead, the president's so-called 'Healthy Forests' initiative exploits the fear of fires in order to gut environmental protections and boost commercial logging. "Instead of focusing on fire-proofing communities, the Bush plan would emphasize logging large and medium trees in remote areas of national forests which does little to protect human life and property. In fact, removing the most fire-resistant trees and building roads in the backcountry may actually increase the risk of catastrophic wildfires.

"The administration is asking Congress to torch our most basic environmental protections in the guise of fire prevention. Rolling back rules for the timber industry and eliminating public participation represent yet another cynical attempt by perhaps the most anti-environmental administration in U.S. history to line the pockets of its corporate friends at the expense of public safety and our natural heritage."

Lie Five: ". . . to meet a severe and urgent crisis abroad, tonight I propose the Emergency Plan for AIDS Relief—a work of mercy beyond all current international efforts to help the people of Africa. This comprehensive plan will prevent seven million new AIDS infections, treat at least two million people with life extending drugs and provide humane care for millions of people suffering from AIDS, and for children orphaned by AIDS."

(Applause)

There was, of course, no plausible Emergency Plan. Worse,

according to a joint study conducted by Population Action International, Planned Parenthood Federation of America, and Ipas (September 24, 2003), the "joint efforts" are being impeded by Bush's reinstatement of the "global gag rule" shortly after he took office of which columnist R. E. Blummer writes in the *St. Petersburg Times* (10/12/03):

> If a population is not going to refrain from sex—the protection against transmission is the best defense. But sub-Saharan Africa, home to 30 million of the world's 40 million HIV/AIDS sufferers is suddenly facing a condom shortage. Family-planning clinics from Ethiopia to Swaziland have had their American-donated supplies sharply reduced or cut off and we can thank our president and his religious-right politics for this. President Bush reinstated the Mexico City policy, also known as the global gag rule: the policy bars organizations that receive U.S. international family-planning funds from having anything to do with abortion; even uttering the word in counseling is verboten.

Bush's "Emergency Plan" has resulted in the shutting down of five clinics in Kenya. And an increase not only in AIDS, but in unsafe abortions, a word not to be whispered in America's deeply religious chigger states, whose every superstition about sex is pandered to by a president eager to scoop up their Electoral College votes to compensate for his loss of the popular American vote in 2000.

Lie Six: "Sending Americans into battle is the most profound decision a president can make. The technologies of war have changed; the risks and the suffering of war have not. For the brave Americans who bear the risk, no victory is free from sorrow." Along with this plangent tribute to our brave boys, the Bush administration has been cutting back on medical benefits heretofore taken for granted.

Washington Times, November 9, 2003. Rep. Chet Edwards, a Democrat, is quoted. "I have great concern that trillion-dollar tax cuts to some of America's wealthiest families have cut into our promise to support a decent quality of life for our military families and health care for our veterans." Mr. Edwards is from the Texas district that includes the huge army base Fort Hood. He accuses Bush and his Republicans in Congress for cuts in military housing and ten-year reduction in veterans' health care. "What message does it send to our veterans when the administration says American taxpayers can afford to build new hospitals in Iraq, but we cannot afford to keep open veterans' hospitals here at home?" Further, 50,000 veterans are now waiting six months or more for an appointment at a Department of Veterans Affairs hospital.

Apropos Lie Six, Bush's unremitting war against the American military and Our Brave Boys, one begins to think that something snapped in him when he evaded service in Vietnam by pretending that he was, from time to time, as his busy schedule allowed, a fly-boy in the Texas/Alabama Air National Guard.

On this subject Dave Lindorff (December 2, 2003, *In These Times*) notes:

Over the last year and a half, President Bush has staged more than a third of his major public events before active military personnel or veterans. His rowdy "Hooahs" and policy pronouncements—even when they have nothing to do with military matters—are predictably greeted with rabid applause.

But those easy and unquestioning crowds at military bases and American Legion halls will be increasingly hard to come by as soldiers and veterans start to notice the string of insults and budget cuts inflicted upon them. Even more than his father, and Ronald Reagan before him, Bush is cutting budgets for myriad programs intended to protect or improve the lives of veterans and active duty soldiers.

Lindorf goes on to inform us:

- With 130,000 soldiers still in the heat of battle in Iraq and more fighting and dying in Afghanistan, the Bush administration sought this year to cut $75 a month from the "imminent danger" pay added to soldiers' paychecks when in battle zones. The administration sought to cut by $150 a month the family separation allowance offered to those same soldiers and others who serve overseas away from their families. Although they were termed "wasteful and unnecessary" by the White House, Congress blocked those cuts this year, largely because of Democratic votes.

- This year's White House budget for Veterans Affairs cut $3 billion from VA hospitals—despite 9,000 casualties in Iraq and as aging Vietnam veterans demand more care; VA spending today averages $2,800 less per patient than nine years ago.

- The administration also proposed levying a $250 annual charge on all Priority 8 veterans—those with "non-service-related" illnesses—who seek treatment at VA facilities, and seeks to close VA hospitals to Priority 8 veterans who earn more than $26,000 a year.

> Until protests led to a policy change, the Bush administration also was charging injured GIs from Iraq $8 a day for food when they arrived for medical treatment at the Fort Stewart, Georgia base where most injured are treated.

> In mid-October, the Pentagon, at the request of Defense Secretary Donald Rumsfeld, announced plans to shutter 19 commissaries—military-run stores that offer discounted food and merchandise that helps low-paid enlisted troops and their families get by—along with the possibility of closing 19 more.

> At the same time, the Pentagon also announced it was trying to determine whether to shutter 58 military-run schools for soldiers' children at 14 military installations.

> The White House is seeking to block a federal judge's award of damages to a group of servicemen who sued the Iraqi government for torture during the 1991 Gulf War. The White House claims the money, to come from Iraqi assets confiscated by the United States, is needed for that country's reconstruction.

> The administration beat back a bipartisan attempt in Congress to add $1.3 billion for VA hospitals to Bush's request of $87 billion for war and reconstruction in Iraq and Afghanistan.

> In perhaps its most dangerous policy, the White House is refusing to provide more than 40,000 active-duty troops in Iraq with Kevlar body armor, leaving it up to them and their families to buy this life-saving

equipment. This last bit of penny-pinching prompted Pentagon critic and Vietnam veteran, Col. David Hackworth, to point to "the cost of the extraordinary security" during Bush's recent visit to Asia, which he noted grimly "would cover a vest for every soldier" in Iraq.

Woody Powell, executive director of Veterans for Peace and a veteran of the Korean War, says these White House efforts should be viewed as attacks against American soldiers. "I don't think they see it as attacking them," he says, "They see it as saving money. But it's the wrong thing to be cutting, just like cutting education is a bad thing." Increasingly, veterans, troops and their families are getting angry. *Army Times,* a newspaper widely read in military circles, ran a June 30 editorial saying: "President Bush and the Republican-controlled Congress have missed no opportunity to heap richly deserved praise on the military. But talk is cheap and getting cheaper by the day, judging by the nickel-and-dime treatment the troops are getting lately." Ronald Conley, commander of the conservative American Legion, also recently blasted the White House for VA budget cuts and surcharges, saying: "This is a raw deal for veterans no matter how you cut it. The administration is sending a message that these vets are not a priority at all."

Bush seems to think that the American military are his toys to play with. He commits them to illegal—that is, preemptive—wars and before victory is won, he wanders off to start another war with a casual disregard for his toys. When he gets around to Syria (apparently the next war on the neocon agenda) he may find himself the first American president to preside over a mutiny.

3

The ever-reckless Cheney-Bush junta has not only created Homeland Security, the USA Patriot Acts and an in-your-face set of foreign and domestic policies that, taken as a whole, suggest that madness is now afoot in the higher political circles. For one thing, Bush seems not to care whether he offends the decent opinion of mankind. He gives tax cuts to friends, thus reducing government revenues, while engaging in what looks to be a series of wars in pursuit, presumably, of most of the world's oil reserves. Although a relatively sane (if perilous) case can be made for nailing down for the United States all fossil fuels (predicted to run out in 2020, according to a report prepared for the vice president by councilors whose names he will not share with Congress) the actual nailing down through preemptive attacks on other nations is a cause of some bewilderment. Not since the 1846 attack on Mexico in order to seize California has an American government been so nakedly predatory. It is as if the cheerleader from the Phillips Academy Andover had, somehow, recently and secretly, drawn a great sword of invincibility from the stone. Certainly, his words and deeds reflect a conviction that he can do anything he likes and win against all odds.

He is like a man in one of those dreams who knows he is safe in bed and so can commit any crime he likes in his voluptuous alternative world. No one can stop him. He will even, he appears to think, be re-elected in November 2004 no matter what. Yet, given the state of our economy, that does give him over a million unemployed citizens to make soldiers of, he is apt to be hugely voted out of office, if that is possible now that balloting can be electronically tallied and falsified. His overall behavior suggests a kind of madness, unless he knows something that we don't, thanks to the Help America Vote Act.

The last time a president went mad in a similar manner was in 1945, when Harry S. Truman learned that our atomic bomb was a success and that even though Japan was ready to surrender, he could now drop one or two bombs on the defeated enemy to impress our new enemy and recent partner in the war against the Axis, Stalin, who would then bow to our will due to our formidable strength. Despite the protests of every senior American military commander from Eisenhower to Nimitz, Truman's imperial policy prevailed. Two Japanese cities were atomized. The cold war began—and lasted for a generation.

So—does Bush hold Arthur's sword Excalibur? Or has he a new weapon that makes him reckless as he gallops through the dry wood, dropping matches? Well, he does have access to something that *could* make him feel invincible. He may well not lose this year's presidential election no matter how many Americans vote against him because of a concerted plan to turn over the nation's voting machines, state by state, to three computer voting-machine manufacturers, Diebold, Sequoia, and Election System and Software (ES&S), whose most ingenious model is one that voters are alleged to love—one where you just touch a screen and the candidate of your choice is supposedly recorded by a black box back of the screen as one vote closer to election.

Unfortunately, evidence to the contrary exists. At various points, between the touch of the screen and the counting of the votes, the vote for your candidate can be reversed so that his opponent gets your vote. If you and other concerned citizens feel that the wrong candidate has won, you would ordinarily go to the local supervisor of elections and ask that the ballot machinery be examined. After all, these are mere computers, vulnerable to hackers—and others. But the three principal supplies-companies have made it a condition of the use of their product that only employees of the manufacturer can ever take a look inside in order "to protect trade secrets." It is not explained how the simple registering and counting of a ballot could involve a trade secret of any kind.

In great detail, Bev Harris, a splendid journalist-patriot, has investigated not only the various machines, but the various CEOs and technicians behind them. I suggest that anyone who is alarmed at how the hijacking of the central power of the people took place—is taking place—read her book, *Black Box Voting* (Plan Nine Publishing).

4

In October 2002, Bush signed the Help America Vote Act (HAVA) providing $3.9 billion to replace the nation's old worn-out punch-card and lever machines with their high error rate. Replacing with what? The three interested companies were ready with Direct Recording Electronic (DRE) systems like the touch screen. There was only one flaw: DREs are less accurate than punch cards; worse, interested parties can program them to overturn the actual vote. Lobbyists for DREs got to many of the state officials. Currently, 40,000 Diebold machines are being used in thirty-seven states. I leave to Bev Harris *details* of what has been—and is being—done to corrupt our voting system.

Some tales of what seems to have been done. In Georgia,

a year ago November, the war hero and Democratic senator Max Cleland was ahead of his Republican rival Saxby Chamblis by 2 to 5 points. The final touch-screen vote gave Chamblis 53 points to Cleland's 46, while Democratic governor Barnes lost to the Republican candidate Perdue 46 percent to 51 percent, a sudden swing of 9 to 12 points. Also, surreal numbers were coming in from around the state. Solid Democratic districts were going Republican, and vice versa. Oh, brave new world! On a lesser scale, odd things were happening in Colorado, Minnesota, Illinois, and New Hampshire. The best account of that ominous election is by Andrew Gumbel in England's *The Independent*.

The American press has generally shied away from telling us about ballot fraud. Almost the first hard news of our electoral misadventures was published in New Zealand. Incidentally, the owners of the three computer companies all prove to be Republicans, while Diebold's chief executive, Walden O'Dell, wrote a fund-raising letter for Republicans, declaring that he was "committed to helping Ohio deliver its electoral votes to the president next year." Hence, W's happy face?

On January 23, the *New York Times* allowed John Schwartz, one of its journalists, to write how

A new $23 million system to allow soldiers and other Americans overseas to vote via the Internet is inherently insecure and should be abandoned, according to a panel of computer security experts asked by the US government to review the program. The system, Secure Electronic Registration and Voting Experiment or SERVE, was developed with financing from the Defense Department and will be first used this year (2004) in the primaries and general election. The authors of the new report noted that computer security experts had voiced extremely strong warnings about the reliability of the electronic voting systems, but said that the new voting program, which allows people overseas to vote from their personal computers over the Internet, raises the ante." Because the 2004 election is crucial to our life as a republic, to impose a deeply flawed voting system under Pentagon auspices seems suicidal.

How are the states responding? California authorities seem aware of the dangers. They have mandated "a paper trail" as proof to the voter and to the ballot-counters that each touch-screen vote was actually registered and totaled properly. Unhappily, this safeguard will not go into effect until July of 2005, long after the damage—if there should be any—is done.

Thus far, the Federal Voting Assistance Program (under Rumsfeld's Pentagon) has signed up Arkansas, Florida, Hawaii, Utah, Washington, North and South Carolina; and 100,000 voters are expected to use the paperless system this year, a system described by *Fortune* magazine as "the worst technology of 2003."

Cynics like to remind us that cheating at election time is an old American tradition.

During Franklin Roosevelt's first successful campaign for the New York State Senate, his wife Eleanor liked to tell this story on herself. After a hard day of canvassing for the Democrats, she hurried home to Hyde Park. "Franklin there are people *buying* votes right here in Dutchess County. I have seen them."

"Don't worry, dear," was the happy warrior's response, "the Republicans are buying them, too."

This is the ultimate fallback position of conspirators: everyone does it. Nixon-admiring *Time* magazine put me on its cover when I published *1876,* a book about the stealing of the election a century earlier, with the knowing caption, "The Sins of the Fathers"—not quite my message, but definitely theirs as murky waters were straining the Watergate. Roosevelt told lies to get us into the war against Hitler which, considering the nature of the beast, many people were and are glad that he did. But he did not lie to cover up his administration's errors, or to make money for his friends, as is the case now. Of course, we were winners then—thanks, in good part, to him. Now we are adrift. What next?

Well, what next seems to have arrived stealthily in the night.

THE PRIVATIZING OF AMERICAN ELECTIONS

Long before Bev Harris and her current revelations of Black Box voting, there was a fascinating study called *VOTESCAM, The Stealing of America* written by two brothers, James M. and Kenneth F. Collier, journalists who were interested in who actually counts the votes that we cast in a presidential year; other times as well. The Colliers quote Dr. Howard Strauss, who sounded the alarm on Dan Rather's *CBS Evening News*. Strauss, a Princeton computer science professor, warned:

> The presidential election of 1992, without too much difficulty and with little chance of the felons getting caught, could be stolen by computers for one candidate or another. The candidate who can win by computer has

worked far enough ahead to rig the election by getting his "consultants" to write the software that runs thousands of vote-counting computers from coast to coast. There are so many computers that use the same software now that a presidential election can be tampered with— in fact, may already be tampered with. Because of trade secrecy, nobody can be the wiser.

In movie-land this is known as a high-concept-thriller plot line. Of course, if it is true . . .

It is true that in 1988, at the time of the New Hampshire primary (unexpectedly won by Bush Senior and lost by Senator Dole) an unofficial private corporation, News Election Services (NES), had actual physical control of the counting of the vote, we are told, and "it refuses to let the public know how it is done." The history of NES arouses suspicion. It was created in 1964 shortly after JFK's murder in order, according to the Colliers, to control the conspiracy theories about Dallas. AP, UPI, CBS, NBC, ABC, and CNN got "from Congress the *exclusive franchise* to count the vote in every state." Yet, magically, without a single actual vote counted, NES on election night proclaims the Presidency just minutes after the polls close while Voter Research and Surveys (VRS), used by a consortium of media that covers exit polls, proclaims the Presidency even before the polls close. The Colliers note that in 1989 "the networks finally admitted that a consortium was formed in which ABC, NBC, CBS and CNN would pool their 'resources' to conduct exit polls;" and VRS was born. Interestingly, VRS and NES "both filter their numbers through the same mainframe computer located on New York City's 34th Street." When the Colliers tried to find out just how the polling was done, Warren Mitofsky, chief of the exit-polling division at CBS, stonewalled them with the mantra: "This is not a proper area of inquiry." They did discover that VRS uses a firm called Chilton Research of Radnor, Pennsylvania. When the Colliers applied for jobs as exit-pollsters "we were told that Chilton employs other subpolling organizations in various states to do the actual hiring of field personnel." No further information was forthcoming. "Mitofsky, VRS and Chilton refuse to explain how they operate by claiming they are private groups and don't have to tell the American people a damn thing." Thus, we were—and are—privatized.

Sooner or later, wherever mischief lurks, a member of the Bush family can be observed on the premises. The Colliers tell us:

> Among the wickedest recent examples of possible computerized fraud vote . . . is the New Hampshire primary that saved George Bush Senior from getting knocked out of the race to the White House.
>
> The Bush campaign of 1988, as historians have since recollected, was filled with CIA-type disinformation operations and deceptions of the sort that America used in Vietnam, Chile and the Soviet Union. Since George Bush was one of the most admired CIA directors in the history of the organization, this was not so surprising.
>
> Yet George Bush stood to lose the Republican Party nomination if he was beaten by Sen. Robert Dole in the snows of New Hampshire. He had suffered a terrible political wound when Dole won big by a show of hands in an unriggable Iowa caucus. Bush came to New Hampshire with all the earmarks of a loser. . . . Political observers were downbeat in their observations of Bush's

chances in the face of Dole's Iowa momentum. Virtually every television and newspaper poll had Bush losing by up to eight points just hours before the balloting. . . . Then came a widely reported promise made by Bush to his campaign manager Gov. Sununu. It happens that Sununu's computer engineering skills approach "genius" on the tests. If Sununu could "deliver" New Hampshire, and Bush didn't care how and didn't want to know how—Sununu then would become his chief of staff in the White House.

Headline in the *Washington Post,* this "was perhaps the most polled primary election in American history." What had happened? We will probably never know. "There was no rechecking of the computerized voting machines, no inquiry into the path of the vote from the voting machines to the central tallying place. . . . Nothing was said in the press about the secretly programmed computer chips inside the Shouptronic Direct Recording Electronic (DRE) voting machines in Manchester, the state's largest city."

The Colliers write of what they found out in the 1990s. Today, in the new millennium, those private companies that control the voting and the tallying systems are still entirely beyond our scrutiny. "No voter, no citizens group, not even any academic group of experts is allowed to examine a voting machine." I am quoting from Andy Stephenson, currently a candidate for secretary of state in Washington State. (If elected, he would be in a position to *try* to investigate the privatizers of our democracy.)

"In addition," he adds, "the process of voter registration is being turned over to proprietary, secret software.

"Whereas vote-rigging has always required physical access before, modems and wireless communication devices now open up possibilities for remote rigging that no one can observe." Stephenson's corrective:

"We must enact legislation to mandate paper ballots that the voter verifies at the polling place when he votes; without the need of an interface or a translation . . . voter-verified paper ballots to be deposited in a secure ballot box; and robust auditing of paper ballots against machine counts." Meanwhile, our national elections are now won and lost on shadowy 34th Street.

II

THREE

THE DAY THE AMERICAN
EMPIRE RAN OUT OF GAS

On September 16, 1985, when the Commerce Department announced that the United States had become a debtor nation, the American Empire was as dead,

theoretically, as its predecessor, the British. Our empire was seventy-one years old and had been in ill financial health since 1968. Like most modern empires, ours rested not so much on military prowess as on economic primacy.★

After the French Revolution, the world money power shifted from Paris to London. For three generations, the British maintained an old-fashioned colonial empire, as well as a modern empire based on London's supremacy in the money markets. Then, in 1914, New York replaced London as the world's financial capital. Before 1914, the United States had been a developing country, dependent on outside investment. But with the shift of the money power from Old World to

★ Could it have been these words of mine that stimulated a small group of radicals, soon to call themselves "neo-conservatives," to conspire to propagandize us toward perpetual war to gain *military* primacy globally to compensate for loss of economic primacy?

New, what had been a debtor nation became a creditor nation and the central motor to the world's economy. All in all, the English were well pleased to have us take their place. They were too few in number for so big a task. As early as the turn of the century, they were eager for us not only to help them out financially, but to continue, on their behalf, the destiny of the Anglo-Saxon race: to bear with courage the white man's burden, as Rudyard Kipling not so tactfully put it. Were we not—English and Americans—all Anglo-Saxons, united by common blood, laws, language? Well, no, we were not. But our differences were not so apparent then. In any case, we took the job. We would supervise and civilize the lesser breeds. We would make money.

By the end of the Second World War, we were the most powerful and least damaged of the great nations. We also had most of the money. America's peaceful hegemony lasted exactly five years. Then the cold and hot wars began. Our masters would have us believe that all our problems are the fault of the Evil Empire of the East, with its satanic and atheistic religion, ever ready to destroy us in the night. This nonsense began at a time when we had atomic weapons and the Russians did not. They had lost twenty million of their people in the war, and eight million of them before the war, thanks to their neoconservative Mongolian political system. Most important, there was never any chance, then or now, of the money power shifting from New York to Moscow.

What was—and is—the reason for the big scare? Well, the Second World War made prosperous the United States, which had been undergoing a depression for a dozen years, and made very rich those magnates and their managers who govern the republic, with many a wink, in the people's name. In order to maintain a general prosperity (and enormous wealth for the few) they decided that we would become the world's policeman, perennial shield against the Mongol hordes. We shall have an arms race, said one of the high priests, John Foster Dulles, and we shall win it because the Russians will go broke first. We were then put on a permanent wartime economy, which is why close to two-thirds of the government's revenues are constantly being siphoned off to pay for what is euphemistically called "defense."

As early as 1950, Albert Einstein understood the nature of the rip-off. He said, "The men who possess real power in the country have no intention of ending the cold war." Thirty-five years later they are still at it, making money while the nation itself declines to eleventh place in world per-capita income, to forty-sixth place in literacy and so on, until last summer (not suddenly, I fear) we found ourselves close to $2 trillion in debt. Then, in the fall, the money power shifted from New York to Tokyo, and that looked to be the end of our empire. Now the long-feared Asiatic colossus takes its turn as the world leader, and we—the white race—have become the yellow man's burden. Let us hope that he will treat us more kindly than we treated him.* In any case, if the foreseeable future is not nuclear, it will be Asiatic, some combination of Japan's advanced technology with China's resourceful landmass. Europe and the United States will then be, simply, irrelevant to the world that matters, and so we come full circle: Europe began as the relatively empty uncivilized Wild West of Asia; then the Western Hemisphere became

---

* Believe it or not, this plain observation was interpreted as a racist invocation of "The Yellow Peril"!

the Wild West of Europe. Now the sun is setting in our West and rising once more in the East.

The British used to say that their empire was obtained in a fit of absentmindedness. They exaggerate, of course; on the other hand, our modem empire was carefully thought out by four men. In 1890 a U.S. Navy captain, Alfred Thayer Mahan, wrote the blueprint for the American imperium, *The Influence of Sea Power Upon History, 1660–1783.* Then Mahan's friend, the historian-geopolitician Brooks Adams, younger brother of Henry, came up with the following formula: "All civilization is centralization. All centralization is economy." He applied the formula in the following syllogism: "Under economical centralization, Asia is cheaper than Europe. The world tends to economic centralization. Therefore, Asia tends to survive and Europe to perish." Ultimately, that is why we were in Vietnam. The amateur historian and professional politician Theodore Roosevelt was much under the influence of Adams and Mahan; he was also their political instrument, most active not so much during his presidency as during the crucial war with Spain, where he can take a good deal of credit for our seizure of the Philippines, which made us a *world* empire. Finally, Senator Henry Cabot Lodge, Roosevelt's closest friend, kept in line a Congress that had a tendency to forget our holy mission—our manifest destiny—and ask, rather wistfully, for internal improvements.

From the beginning of our republic, we have had imperial longings. We took care—as we continue to take care—of the indigenous American population. We maintained slavery a bit too long, even by a cynical world's tolerant standards. Then, in 1846, we produced our first conquistador, President James K. Polk. After acquiring Texas, Polk deliberately started a war with Mexico because, as he later told the historian George Bancroft, we had to acquire California. Thanks to Polk, we did. And that is why to this day the Mexicans refer to our southwestern states as "the occupied lands," which Hispanics are now, quite sensibly, filling up.

The case against empire began as early as 1847. Representative Abraham Lincoln did not think much of Polk's war, while Lieutenant Ulysses S. Grant, who fought at Veracruz, said in his memoirs, "The war was an instance of a republic following the bad example of European monarchies, in not considering the justice in their desire to acquire additional territory." He went on to make a causal link, something not usual in our politics then and completely unknown now: "The Southern rebellion was largely the outgrowth of the Mexican War. Nations, like individuals, are punished for their transgressions. We got our punishment in the most sanguinary and expensive war of modern times."

But the empire has always had more supporters than opponents. By 1895 we had filled up our section of North America. We had tried twice—and failed—to conquer Canada. We had taken everything that we wanted from Mexico. Where next? Well, there was the Caribbean at our front door and the vast Pacific at our back. Enter the Four Horsemen—Mahan, Adams, Roosevelt, and Lodge.

The original republic was thought out carefully, and openly, in *The Federalist Papers*: We were not going to have a monarchy, and we were not going to have a democracy. And to this day we have had neither. For two hundred years we have had an oligarchical system in which men of property can do well and others are on their own. Or, as Brooks Adams put it, the sole problem of our ruling class is whether to coerce or bribe the powerless majority. The so-called Great Society bribed; today coercion is very much in the air. Happily, our neoconservative Mongoloids favor authoritarian if not totalitarian means of coercion.

Unlike the republic, the empire was worked out largely in secret. Captain Mahan, in a series of lectures delivered at the Naval War College, compared the United States with England. Each was essentially an island state that could prevail in the world only through sea power. England had already proved his thesis. Now the United States must do the same. We must build a great navy in order to acquire overseas possessions. Since great navies are expensive, the wealth of new colonies must be used to pay for our fleets. In fact, the more colonies acquired, the more ships; the more ships, the more empire. Mahan's thesis is agreeably circular. He showed how small England has ended up with most of Africa and all of southern Asia, thanks to sea power. He thought that we should do the same. The Caribbean was our first and easiest target. Then on to the Pacific Ocean, with all its islands. And, finally, to China, which was breaking up as a political entity.

Theodore Roosevelt and Brooks Adams were tremendously excited by this prospect. At the time, Roosevelt was a mere police commissioner in New York City, but he had dreams of imperial glory. "He wants to be," snarled Henry Adams, "our Dutch-American Napoleon." Roosevelt began to maneuver his way toward the heart of power, sea power. With Lodge's help, he got himself appointed assistant secretary of the navy, under a weak secretary and a mild president. Now he was in place to modernize the fleet and acquire colonies. Hawaii was annexed. Then a part of Samoa. Finally, colonial

Cuba, somehow, had to be liberated from Spain's tyranny. At the Naval War College, Roosevelt declared, "to prepare for war is the most effectual means to promote peace." How familiar that sounds! But since the United States had no enemies as of June 1897, a contemporary might have remarked that since we were already at peace with everyone, why prepare for war? Today, of course, we are what he dreamed we would be, a nation armed to the teeth, hostile to everyone and eager to strike preemptively, at presidential command. But what with Roosevelt was a design to acquire an empire is for us a means to transfer money from the Treasury to the various defense industries which, in turn, pay for the elections of Congress and president.

Our turn-of-the-century imperialists may have been wrong, and I think they were. But they were intelligent men with a plan, and the plan worked. Aided by Lodge in the Senate, Brooks Adams in the press, Admiral Mahan at the Naval War College, the young assistant secretary of the navy began to build up the fleet and look for enemies. After all, as Brooks Adams proclaimed, "war is the solvent." But war with whom? And for what? And where? At one point England seemed a likely enemy. There was a boundary dispute over Venezuela, which meant that we could invoke the all-purpose Monroe Doctrine (the invention of John Quincy Adams, Brooks's grandfather). But as we might have lost such a war, nothing happened. Nevertheless, Roosevelt kept on beating his drum: "No triumph of peace," he shouted, "can equal the armed triumph of war." Also: "We must take Hawaii in the interests of the white race." Even Henry Adams, who found T.R. tiresome and Brooks, his own brother, brilliant but mad, suddenly declared, "In another fifty years . . . the white race will have to reconquer the tropics by war and nomadic invasion, or be shut up north of the 50th parallel." And so at the century's end, our most distinguished ancestral voices were not prophesying, but praying for war.

An American warship, the *Maine,* blew up in Havana harbor. We held Spain responsible; thus, we got what John Hay called "a splendid little war." We would liberate Cuba, drive Spain from the Caribbean. As for the Pacific, even before the *Maine* was sunk, Roosevelt had ordered Commodore Dewey and his fleet to the Spanish Philippines—just in case. Spain promptly collapsed, and we inherited its Pacific and Caribbean colonies. Admiral Mahan's plan was working triumphantly.

In time we allowed Cuba the appearance of freedom while holding on to Puerto Rico. Then President William McKinley, after an in-depth talk with God, decided that we should also keep the Philippines, in order, he said, to Christianize them. When reminded that the Filipinos were Roman Catholics, the president said, Exactly. We must Christianize them. Although Philippine nationalists had been our allies against Spain, we promptly betrayed them and their leader, Emilio Aguinaldo. As a result it took us several years to conquer the Philippines, and tens—some say hundreds—of thousands of Filipinos died that our empire might grow.

The war was the making of Theodore Roosevelt. Surrounded by the flower of the American press, he led a group of so-called Rough Riders up a very small hill in Cuba. As a result of this proto-photo opportunity he became a national hero, governor of New York, McKinley's running mate and, when McKinley was killed in 1901, president.

Not everyone liked the new empire. After Manila, Mark Twain though that the stars and bars of the American flag should be replaced by a skull and crossbones. He also said, "We cannot maintain an empire in the Orient and maintain a republic in America." He was right, of course. But as he was only a writer who said funny things, he was ignored. The compulsively vigorous Roosevelt defended our war against the Philippine population, and he attacked the likes of Twain. "Every argument that can be made for the Filipinos could be made for the Apaches," he explained, with his lovely gift for analogy. "And every word that can be said for Aguinaldo could be said for Sitting Bull. As peace, order and prosperity followed our expansion over the land of the Indians, so they will follow us in the Philippines."

Despite the criticism of the few, the Four Horsemen had pulled it off. The United States was a world empire. And one of the horsemen not only got to be president but, for his pious meddling in the Russo-Japanese conflict, our greatest apostle of war was awarded the Nobel Peace Prize. One must never underestimate Scandinavian wit.

Empires are restless organisms. They must constantly renew themselves; should an empire start leaking energy, it will die. Not for nothing were the Adams brothers fascinated by entropy. By energy. By force. Brooks Adams, as usual, said the unsayable: "Laws are a necessity," he declared. "Laws are made by the strongest and they must and shall be obeyed." Oliver Wendell Holmes, Jr., thought this a wonderful observation, while the philosopher William James came to a similar conclusion, which can also be detected, like an invisible dynamo, at the heart of the novels of his brother Henry.

According to Brooks Adams, "The most difficult problem of modern times is unquestionably how to protect property under popular governments." The Four Horsemen fretted a lot about this. They need not have. We have never had a popular government in the sense that they feared, nor are we in any danger now. Our only political party has two right wings, one called Republican, the other Democratic. But Henry Adams figured all that out back in the 1890s. "We have a single system," he wrote, and "in that system the only question is the price at which the proletariat is to be bought and sold, the bread and circuses." But none of this was for public consumption. Publicly, the Four Horsemen and their outriders spoke of the American mission to bring all the world freedom and peace—through slavery and war, if necessary. Privately, their constant fear was that the weak masses might combine one day against the strong few, their natural leaders, and take away their money. As early as the election of 1876, socialism had been targeted as a vast evil that must never be allowed to corrupt simple American persons. When Christianity was invoked as the natural enemy of those who might limit the rich and their games, the combination of cross and dollar sign proved—and proves—irresistible.

During the first decade of the disagreeable twentieth century, the great world fact was the internal collapse of China. Who could pick up the pieces? Britain grabbed Kowloon; Russia was busy in the north; the Kaiser's fleet prowled the China coast; Japan was modernizing itself and biding its time. Although Theodore Roosevelt lived and died a dedicated racist, the Japanese puzzled him. After they sank the Russian fleet, Roosevelt decided that they were to be respected and feared even though they were our racial inferiors. For those Americans who served in the Second World War, it was an article of faith—as of 1941, anyway—that the Japanese could never win a modern war. Because of their slant eyes, they would not be able to master aircraft. Then they sank our fleet at Pearl Harbor.

Jingoism aside, Brooks Adams was a good analyst. In the 1890s he wrote:"Russia, to survive, must undergo a social revolution internally and/or expand externally. She will try to move into Shansi Province, richest prize in the world. Should Russia and Germany combine . . ."That was the nightmare of the Four Horsemen. At a time when simpler folk feared the rise of Germany alone, Brooks Adams saw the world ultimately polarized between Russia and the United States, with China as the common prize. American maritime power versus Russia's landmass. That is why, quite seriously, he wanted to extend the Monroe Doctrine to the Pacific Ocean. For him, "War [was] the ultimate form of economic competition."

We are now at the end of the twentieth century. England, France, and Germany have all disappeared from the imperial stage. China is now reassembling itself, and Confucius, greatest of all political thinkers, is again at the center of the Middle Kingdom. Japan has the world money power but needs a landmass; China now seems ready to go into business with its ancient enemy. Wars of the sort that the Four Horsemen enjoyed are, if no longer possible, no longer practical.* Today's true conquests are shifts of currency by computer and the manufacture of those things that people everywhere are willing to buy.

I have said very little about writers because writers have figured very little in our imperial story. The founders of both republic and empire wrote well: Jefferson and Hamilton, Lincoln and Grant, T.R. and the Adamses. Today public figures can

---

* Our ongoing failures in Iraq and Afghanistan prove this fact.

no longer write their own speeches or books, and there is some evidence that they can't read them, either.

Yet at the dawn of the empire, for a brief instant, our *professional* writers tended to make a difference. Upton Sinclair and company attacked the excesses of the ruling class. Theodore Roosevelt coined the word "muckraking" to describe what they were doing. He did not mean the word as praise. Since then a few of our writers have written on public themes, but as they are not taken seriously, they have ended by not taking themselves seriously, at least as citizens of a republic. After all, most writers are paid by universities, and it is not wise to be thought critical of a garrison state which spends so much money on so many campuses.

When Confucius was asked what would be the first thing that he would do if he were to lead the state—a never-to-be-fulfilled dream—he said, *Rectify the language*. This is wise. This is subtle. As societies grow decadent, the language grows decadent, too. Words are used to disguise, not to illuminate, action: You liberate a city by destroying it. Words are used to confuse, so that at election time people will solemnly vote against their own interests. Finally, words must be so twisted as to justify an empire that has now ceased to exist, much less make sense. Is rectification of our system possible for us? Henry Adams thought not. In 1910 he wrote: "The whole fabric of society will go to wrack if we really lay hands of reform on our rotten institutions." Then he added, "From top to bottom the whole system is a fraud, all of us know it, laborers and capitalists alike, and all of us are consenting parties to it." Since then consent has grown frayed; we have become poor; our people sullen.

To maintain a thirty-five-year arms race it is necessary to have a fearsome enemy. Not since the invention of the Wizard of Oz have American publicists created anything quite so demented as the idea that the Soviet Union is a monolithic, omnipotent empire with tentacles everywhere on earth, intent on our destruction, which will surely take place unless we constantly imitate it with *our* war machine and secret services.

In actual fact, the Soviet Union is a Second World country with a First World military capacity. Frighten the Russians sufficiently and they might blow us up. By the same token, as our republic now begins to crack under the vast expense of maintaining a mindless imperial force, *we* might try to blow *them* up. Particularly if we had a president who really was a twice-born Christian and believed that the good folks would all go to heaven (where they were headed anyway) and the bad folks would go where *they* belong.

Even worse than the not-very-likely prospect of a nuclear war—deliberate or by accident—is the economic collapse of our society because too many of our resources have been wasted on the military. The Pentagon is like a black hole; what goes in is forever lost to us, and no new wealth is created. Hence, our cities, whose centers are unlivable; our crime rate, the highest in the Western world; a public education system that has given up . . . you know the litany.

There is now only one way out. The time has come for the United States to make common cause with the Soviet Union. The bringing together of the Soviet landmass (with all its natural resources) and our island empire (with all its technological resources) would be of great benefit to each society, not to mention the world. Also, to recall the wisdom of the Four Horsemen who gave us our empire, the Soviet Union and our section of North America combined would be a match, industrially and technologically, for the Sino-Japanese axis that will dominate the future just as Japan dominates world trade as of today. But where the horsemen thought of war as the supreme solvent, we now know that war is worse than useless. Therefore, the alliance of the two great powers of the Northern Hemisphere will double the strength of each and give us, working together, an opportunity to survive, economically, in a highly centralized Asiatic world.★

—*The Nation*
January 11, 1986

★ The suggestion that the United States and the USSR join forces set alarm bells ringing in Freedom's Land. The Israel lobby, in particular.

FOUR

A CHEERFUL RESPONSE

Recently, Norman Mailer and I chatted together at the Royale Theatre in New York, under the auspices of the PEN American Center. Part of what I said was

reprinted in *The Nation* on January 11, 1986. I gave a bit of a history lesson about our empire's genesis, and I brooded on its terminus last fall, when Tokyo took over from New York as the world's economic center.

My conclusion: For America to survive economically in the coming Sino-Japanese world, an alliance with the Soviet Union is a necessity. After all, the white race is a minority race with many well-deserved enemies, and if the two great powers of the Northern Hemisphere don't band together, we are going to end up as farmers—or, worse, mere entertainment—for more than one billion grimly efficient Asiatics.[*]

---

[*] Again, I was attacked as a racist, invoking the "Yellow Peril." Simultaneously, the Japanese premier announced that the United States was a failure because there were too many inferior races in our heterodox land, while one of his cabinet ministers predicted that, in the next century, the United States would be Japan's farm, and Western Europe its boutique.

As expected, that wonderful, wacky couple, Norman (Poddy) Podhoretz and his wife, Midge Decter, checked in. The Lunts of the right wing (Israeli Likudite), they are now, in their old age, more and more like refugees from a Woody Allen film: *The Purple Prose of West End Avenue.*

Poddy was the first to respond. He is the editor of *Commentary* (circulation 55,000 and allegedly falling; paid for by the American Jewish Committee). He is best known—and by me loved—for his autobiographical "novel," *Making It,* in which he tells us that he has made it because he has become editor of *Commentary* and might one day be a guest at the White House, as he has already been a guest of Huntingdon Hartford in Nassau. Over the years, Poddy has, like his employers, the AJC, moved from those liberal positions traditionally occupied by American Jews (and me) to the far right of American politics. The reason for that is simple. In order to get Treasury money for Israel (last year $5 billion), pro-Israel lobbyists must see to it that America's "the Russians are coming" squads are in place so that they can continue to frighten the American people into spending enormous sums for "defense," which also means the support of Israel in its never-ending wars against just about everyone. To make sure that nearly two-thirds of the federal budget goes to the Pentagon and Israel, it is necessary for the pro-Israel lobbyists to make common cause with our lunatic right. Hence, the virulent propaganda.

Poddy denounced Mailer and me in the pages of the *New York Post.* According to him, we belong to that mindless majority of pinko intellectuals who actually think that the nation spends too much on the Pentagon and not enough on, say, education. Since sustained argument is not really his bag, he must fall back on the *ad hominem* attack, a right-wing specialty—and, of course, on our flag, which he wears like a designer caftan because "the blessings of freedom and prosperity are greater and more widely shared [here] than in any country known to human history." Poddy should visit those Western European countries whose per capita income is higher than ours. All in all, Poddy is a silly billy.

Significantly, the one Yiddish word that has gained universal acceptance in this country is *chutzpah*. Example: In 1960, Mr. and Mrs. Podhoretz were in upstate New York where I used to live. I was trying out a play at the Hyde Park Playhouse; the play was set during the Civil War. "Why," asked Poddy, "are you writing a play about, of all things, the Civil War?" I explained to him that my mother's family had fought for the Confederacy and my father's for the Union, and that the Civil War was—and is—to the United States what the Trojan War was to the Greeks; the great single tragic event that continues to give resonance to our Republic.

"Well, to me," said Poddy, "the Civil War is as remote and as irrelevant as the War of the Roses." I realized then that he was not planning to become an "assimilated American," to use the old-fashioned terminology; but, rather, his first loyalty would always be to Israel. Yet he and Midge stay on among us, in order to make propaganda and raise money for Israel—a country they don't seem eager to live in. Jewish joke, circa 1900: A Zionist is someone who wants to ship other people off to Palestine.

Midge was next to strike. But before she launched her attack, in something called *Contentions,* she put on her thinking cap and actually read what I wrote. I give her high marks for that. Unfortunately, she found my history lesson hard going. But then, like most of our Israeli fifth columnists, Midge isn't much interested in what the *goyim* were up to before Ellis Island. She also likes the *ad hominem* attack. When I noted that our writers seldom speak out on matters of war and peace because so many of them are paid for by universities that receive money from the garrison state, Midge tartly retorted, *"He,* after all, is not paid by a university but by those great centers of independence, the film companies." Since my last Hollywood film, *The Best Man,* was made in 1964, I have been "paid" by that American public that buy my books about the American past, a subject of no demonstrable interest to Midge and Poddy and their friends.

Midge was amazed by my description of how we seized territories from Mexico, including California; annexed Hawaii and Puerto Rico, and, of course, the Philippines, where we slaughtered between 100,000 and 200,000 of the inhabitants. Interesting note: American imperialists froth if the figures for those murdered are ever in excess of 60,000 men, women, and children, the acceptable statistical minimum for genocide. Then Midge, with that magisterial gooniness that marks her polemical style, told us, "that three of these conquered territories are now states of the United States, and a fourth an independent republic, is evidently beside the point—as, we cannot resist remarking . . ."

Oh, Midge, resist. Resist! Don't you get the point? We stole other people's land. We murdered many inhabitants. We imposed our religion—and rule—on the survivors. General Grant was ashamed of what we did to Mexico, and so am I. Mark Twain was ashamed of what we did in the Philippines, and so am I. Midge is not because in the Middle East another predatory people is busy stealing other people's land in the name of an alien theocracy. She is a propagandist for these predators (paid for?), and that is what all this nonsense is about.

Since spades may not be called spades in freedom's land, let me spell it all out. In order to get military and economic support for Israel, a small number of American Jews,* who should know better, have made common cause with every sort of reactionary and anti-Semitic group in the United States, from the corridors of the Pentagon to the TV studios of the evangelical Jesus Christers. To show that their hearts are in the far-right place, they call themselves "neo–conservatives" and attack the likes of Mailer and me, all in the interest of supporting the likes of Sharon and Greater Israel as opposed to the Peace Now Israelis, whom they disdain. There is real madness here; mischief, too.

"Well, one thing is clear in all this muddle," writes Midge, adrift in her tautological sea, "Mr. Vidal does not like his country." Poor Midge. Of course I like my country. After all, I'm its current biographer.

Although there is nothing wrong with being a lobbyist for a foreign power, one is supposed to register with the Justice Department. Also, I should think that tact would require a certain forbearance when it comes to the politics of the host country. But tact is unknown to the Podhoretzes. Joyously, they revel in the politics of hate, with harsh attacks on blacks and/or fags and/or liberals, trying, always, to outdo those Christian moral majoritarians who will, as Armageddon draws

---

* This sentence has since been carefully revised by publicists like W. Safire and M. Peretz and C. Krauthammer to mean "all Jews," thus demonstrating my "virulent" anti-Semitism. Well, ours is a sectarian society.

near, either convert the Jews, just as the Good Book says, or kill them.

All in all, the latest Podhoretz diatribes have finally convinced me that the time has come for the United States to stop all aid not only to Israel, but to Jordan, Egypt, and the rest of the Arab world. The Middle Easterners would then be obliged to make peace, or blow one another up, or whatever. In any case, we would be well out of it. After all, the theological and territorial quarrels of Israel and Islam are as remote to 225 million Americans as—what else?—the War of the Roses.

—*The Nation*
March 22, 1986

FIVE

ARMAGEDDON?

I

As the curtain falls on the ancient Acting President and his "Administration," it is time to analyze just what this bizarre episode in American history was all about.

When Ronald Reagan's career in show business came to an end, he was hired to impersonate, first, a California governor, and then an American president who would reduce taxes for his employers, the southern and western New Rich, much of whose money came from the defense industries. There is nothing unusual in this arrangement. All recent presidents have had their price tags, and the shelf life of each was short. What was unusual was his employers' cynical recognition that in an age of television one must steer clear of politicians who may not know how to act president and go instead for the best actor available for the job, the one who can read with warm plausibility the commercials that they have written for him.

Now it is quite possible to find an actor who does understand politics. Orson Welles and Gregory Peck come to mind; but would they have been sufficiently malleable? The producers were not about to experiment. They selected an actor who has never shown the slightest interest in actual politics as opposed to the mechanics of political elections in the age of television. That is why Reagan's economic and foreign policies have never made the slightest sense to anyone who knows anything about either. On the other hand, there is evidence that, unlike his wealthy sponsors, he has a sense of mission that, like Jesus', is not of this world.

The Great Obfuscator has come among us to dispense not only good news for the usual purposes of election, but Good News. Reagan is nothing so mundane as an American president. Rather, he is here to prepare us for the coming war between the Christ and the Antichrist. A war, to be specific, between the United States and Russia, to take place in Israel. Hence, the mysterious and irrelevant, to most of us, exhortations about prayer in the schools, abortion, drugs, evil empires and, most lately, the encroaching "sea of darkness." Hence, the military buildup that can never, ever cease until we have done battle for the Lord. Hence, the evangelical tone which makes the priestly eloquence of the late Woodrow Wilson sound like the current mayor of New York City. Hence, the perfect indifference to the disintegration of the American economy, educational system, industrial infrastructure; and, finally, really finally, the all-out one-time-only investment in a nuclear war to end all wars and Evil itself. The world is simply a used-up Kleenex, as Reagan's secretary of the interior, James Watt, acknowledged when he scorned the environmentalists with the first hint of what was in the works: "I do not know," he said to Congress in 1981, "how many future generations we can count on before the Lord returns." So why conserve anything, if Judgment Day is at hand?

For those, and I am one, who have been totally mystified

by this president's weird indifference to the general welfare at
home and the preservation of peace abroad, the most plausible
answer has now been given in a carefully documented and
deeply alarming book called *Prophecy and Politics: Militant
Evangelists on the Road to Nuclear War*. The Texas-born author,
Grace Halsell, comes from a fundamentalist Christian family.
She has been for many years a working journalist, the author
of seven books, a speechwriter for Lyndon Johnson, and a
longtime student of the twice-born Christians and their current president.

According to Halsell's interpretation and synthesis of facts
available to all, the old actor has been rehearsing for some time
the part of the Great Anarch who lets the curtain fall on the
late great planet earth, as prophesied in the Good Book and in
that even Better Book, *The Late Great Planet Earth* by Hal
Lindsey, an ex-riverboat captain, whose account of the ultimate showdown between Christ and Antichrist was much
admired by Ronald Reagan as well as by the 18 million other
Christian fundamentalists who bought the book in the 1970s
and who believe that we are living in the penultimate Dispensation. The what? Let me explain.

Let us begin not with the Old Testament sky-god but with
one Clyde Ingerson Scofield, who was born in Michigan in
1843. Scofield had an innate end-of-the-world bent which was
reinforced by an Anglo-Irish divine named John Nelson Darby,
who "taught that God had two plans and two groups of people
with whom to work. Israel was God's kingdom here on earth
and the Church (Christianity) was God's heavenly kingdom."
According to Scofield/Darby the sky-god has divided history
into seven seven-year plans, or "Dispensations." During each
Dispensation, God relates to man in a different way. Obviously,

this particular sky-god is highly bureaucratic, even Leninist in his approach. Although Scofield was easily able to identify seven Dispensations in scripture, others could not. Eager to shed light, Mr. Scofield then sat down and rewrote the Bible so that we could all share in the Bad News. In 1909, he published the first *Scofield Reference Bible*. Since then many millions of copies of his mock Bible have been (and are being) sold.

Essentially, the Scofield exegesis is both Manichean (material world evil, spirit good; therefore, man cannot live at peace, is flawed, doomed) and Zoroastrian (Ahura Mazda, the wise Lord, defeats the evil Ahriman at the end of "the time of long dominion"). During the last-but-one Dispensation, Christ will defeat the Antichrist at Armageddon, fifty-five miles north of Tel Aviv. Just before the battle, the Church will be wafted to Heaven and all the good folks will experience "Rapture," as Scofield calls it. The wicked will suffer horribly. Then, after seven years of "burying the dead" (presumably there will be survivors), God returns, bringing Peace and Joy and the Raptured Ones.

The gospel according to Scofield is preached daily by such American television divines as Jerry Falwell, Pat Robertson, Jimmy Swaggart, Jim Bakker, *et al.*, and according to a Yankelovich poll (1984), 39 percent of the American people believe in the death of the earth by nuclear fire; and Rapture. Among the 39 percent is Ronald Reagan, as we shall see.

In 1985, Grace Halsell went on a Falwell Old Time Gospel Hour Tour of the Holy Land. If any of the good Christians on this tour expected to gaze upon Bethlehem and Nazareth where their God's son was born and lived, they were doomed to disappointment. These trips have only one purpose: to raise money for Falwell and Israel, under the guise of preparing the pilgrims for the approaching Armageddon. At Halsell's request, her group finally met one nervous taciturn local Christian. Moslems were ignored. On the other hand, there were constant briefings by Israelis on their military might.

The Falwell indoctrination is, relentlessly, the imminent end of the world, the ambiguity of the role of the Jews (*why* won't they convert?), and the importance of the state of Israel whose invention in 1948 and victories in 1967 were all foretold, most excitingly, by Scofield: exciting because Dispensationalists can never be sure which Dispensation they happen to be living in. Is this the one that will end in Armageddon? If so, when will the seven years be up and the fireworks start? In 1982, poor Pat Robertson got out on a limb when he thought that Israel's invasion of Lebanon was the beginning of the longed-for end; rapturously, Pat declared on television: "The whole thing is in place now, it can happen at any time. . . . But by fall, undoubtedly something like this will happen which will fulfill Ezekiel." Happily for us, unhappily for Pat, 1982 wasn't the year. But I reckon if we all pray hard enough the end's bound to come real fast.

As Halsell and group gaze upon Armageddon, an innocent rural countryside, one of her companions fills her in on *the meaning of it all*. Reverently, he quotes St. John: "And he gathered them together into a place called in the Hebrew tongue Armageddon." When she inquires what this neutral sentence has to do with a final battle between Christ and Antichrist, she gets a barrage of Bronze Age quotes: "The cities of the nation fell . . . and every island fled away and the mountains were not found." Apparently, the Euphrates then dries up and the Antichrist himself (you guessed it, Gorbachev) crosses into Israel to do battle with the Lord, who comes down from

Heaven, with "a great shout" (played by Charlton Heston—once again, Ronald Reagan is, in Jack Warner's phrase, the star's "best friend"). The Lord and the Americans win hands down, thanks to SDI and the B-I bomber and the Fourteenth Regiment cavalry from Des Moines, Iowa, and a number of Republican elephants who happen to have strayed onto the field, trumpeting free enterprise, as the Lord requires.

Dispensationalists delight in the horror of this crucial (pun intended) battle, as predicted so gloatingly by Ezekiel: "Torrential rains and hailstone, fire and brimstone . . . a great shaking in the land . . . every kind of terror." But it is sly prescient old Zechariah, eye glued to that Bronze Age crystal ball, who foretells atomic weapons: "Their flesh shall consume away while they stand upon their feet, and their eyes shall consume away in their holes, and their tongue shall consume away in their mouth."

What about the Jews? asked Halsell. Since they won't be with Gorbachev (a.k.a. Gog and Magog), what happens to them? The answer is stern: "Two-thirds of all the Jews living here will be killed. . . ." She asks, why, if the Jews are *His* chosen people, as the Dispensationalists believe? The answer glows with charity: "He's doing it mainly for his ancient people, the Jews. . . . He devised a seven-year Tribulation period mainly to purge the Jews, to get them to see the light and recognize Christ as their Savior. . . . Don't you see? God wants them to bow down before His only son, who is our Lord Jesus Christ." Anyway, forget the Jews because many, many other people will also be exterminated so that Christ may come again, *in peace.* Just why Jesus' Dad should have chosen nuclear war as the means of universal peace is as rare and impenetrable a mystery as the Trinity itself.

Although the three religions (Judaism, Christianity, and Islam) of the Book, as Moslems call the Old Testament, are alike in a common worship of a highly primitive sky-god (rejected by the more civilized Hindus, Buddhists, and Confucians) and variously adapted to different times, peoples, and climates, only Fundamentalist Christianity in our century has got so seriously into the end-of-the-world game, or Rapture, as it is described by the Dispensationalists who believe . . .

But why am *I* telling you this? Let Jerry Falwell, the millionaire divine of Lynchburg, Virginia, explain it to you as he did to the journalist Bob Scheer in the *Los Angeles Times* (March 4, 1981): "We believe that Russia, because of her need of oil—and she's running out now [no, she's not, Jerry, *we* are]—is going to move in the Middle East, and particularly Israel because of their hatred of the Jew [so where's the oil there, Jerry?] and that it is at that time when all hell will break out. And it is at that time when I believe there will be some nuclear holocaust on this earth. . . ." Falwell then does the obligatory mishmash from Apocrypha—and the wild "real" thing, too: Russia, "will be ultimately totally destroyed," he tells us. When Scheer says that if that happens the whole world will be destroyed, Falwell spells out the Dispensationalist doctrine: "No, not the whole world, because then our Lord is coming back to the earth. First, he comes to take the Church out [plainly, Falwell was never in the army—for us "to take out" means destroy; he means lift up, save]. Seven years later, after Armageddon, this terrible holocaust, He's coming back to this very earth so it won't be destroyed, and the Church is coming with him [up, down; out, in—the vertiginous Church], to rule and reign with Christ on the earth for a thousand years. . . ." A joyous millennium of no abortion, no sodomy, no crack, no Pure Drug and Food Act, no civil rights, but of schools where only prayers are said, and earth proved daily flat.

"We believe," says Falwell, "we're living in those days just prior to the Lord's coming."When Scheer asks for an expected time of arrival, Falwell assures him that although the Lord has warned them not to give dates, he himself has a hunch: "I do not think we have fifty years left. I don't think my children will live their full lives out . . ." So we are now in the penultimate seven-year Dispensation, which will end with Armageddon.

Scheer suggests that after the nuclear weapons we drop on Russia and the ones they drop on us, the great planet earth will be very late indeed. But Falwell *knows* that there will be survivors, in addition to the taken-out Church. Personally, he has no fear of the nuclear holocaust because, as he said to Halsell's group, with a grin, "You know why I'm not worried? I ain't gonna be here."

2

Halsell notes: "A Nielsen survey released in October 1985 shows that 61 million Americans (40 percent of all regular viewers) listen to preachers who tell them that we can do nothing to prevent a nuclear war in our lifetime." But do the 61 million actually believe what they hear? I suspect that they probably do on the ground that so little other information gets to them. They are not book readers (the United States has dropped to twenty-fourth place among book-reading nations); the public educational system has been allowed to deteriorate as public money goes mostly to defense; while television news is simply entertainment and the principal entertainer (until the latest Iran scandal) is a professional actor who knows very little about anything other than his necessary craft, which is to sell emotions—and Armageddon. But, again, does the salesman believe in the product that he sells? Halsell thinks that he does.

On September 20, 1970, an evangelical Christian, George Otis, and several like-minded folk visited Reagan when he was governor of California. They spoke rapturously of Rapture. Then, according to Otis, they all joined hands in prayer and Otis prophesied Reagan's coming election to the presidency. According to Otis *(Visit with a King),* Reagan's arms "shook and pulsated" during this prophecy. The next summer (June 29, 1971) Reagan asked Billy Graham to address the California legislature; afterward, at lunch, Reagan asked Graham, "Well, do you believe that Jesus Christ is coming soon, and what are the signs of his coming if that is the case?" Graham did not beat about this burning bush. "The indication," he said, "is that Jesus Christ is at the very door."

Later in 1971, Governor Reagan attended a dinner where he sat next to James Mills, the president of the California State Senate. Mills was so impressed by the dinner conversation that he wrote it all down immediately afterward, but published it much later *(San Diego Magazine,* August 1985), *pro bono publico,* if a bit late.

After the main course, the lights dimmed and the flaming bowls of cherries jubilee were served. No doubt inspired by the darkness and the flames, Reagan suddenly asked, out of right field, if Mills had read "the fierce Old Testament prophet Ezekiel." Mills allowed that he had (after all, you don't get

elected to the California State Senate if you say no); as it
turned out, he did know Ezekiel. Then, "with firelit intensity,"
Reagan began to talk about how Libya had now gone communist,* just as Ezekiel had foretold, and "that's a sign that the
day of Armageddon isn't far off." When Mills reminded him
that Ethiopia was also due to go over to Satan and he couldn't,
somehow, see the Emperor Haile Selassie turning pinko or
allowing the Reds to take over his country in order to make
war "on God's Chosen People," Reagan agreed "that everything hasn't fallen into place yet. But there is only that one
thing left that has to happen. The Reds have to take over
Ethiopia." Mills thought this unlikely. Reagan thought it
inevitable: "It's necessary to fulfill the prophecy that Ethiopia
will be one of the ungodly nations that go against Israel." As it
turned out, Reagan was right on target. Three years later,
Ethiopia went communist, or something very like it.

Mills was particularly impressed by Reagan's manner,
which is unusually amiable to the point of goofiness: Now he
was "like a preacher [talking] to a skeptical college student."
Reagan then told Mills: "All of the other prophecies that had
to be fulfilled before Armageddon have come to pass. In the
thirty-eighth chapter of Ezekiel it says God will take the children of Israel from among the heathen when they'd been scat-
tered and will gather them again in the promised land. That
has finally come about after 2,000 years. For the first time ever,
everything is in place for the battle of Armageddon and the
Second Coming of Christ."

When Mills said that the Bible clearly states that men will

---

* Now "communist" Libya is a valued ally of the Bush administration. Is the
Good Lord making fun of us?

never have the fun of knowing just *when* this awesome event will take place, Reagan replied:

> Everything is falling into place. It can't be too long now. Ezekiel says that fire and brimstone will be rained upon the enemies of God's people. That must mean that they will be destroyed by nuclear weapons. . . . Ezekiel tells us that Gog, the nation that will lead all of the other powers of darkness ["sea of darkness," he moaned just after he plunged into Irangate] against Israel, will come out of the north. What other powerful nation is to the north of Israel? None. But it didn't seem to make much sense before the Russian revolution, when Russia was a Christian country. Now it does, now that Russia has become communistic and atheistic, now that Russia has set itself against God. Now it fits the description perfectly.

So you thought there would be an arms deal with the Soviet Union? A cutback of nuclear weapons? Not on, literally, our lives. To stop the arms race would be to give the victory to Gog.

Mills's conversation took place fifteen years ago. Nine years later, the nemesis of Gog was elected president. If he survives, Constitutionally or constitutionally, he has two more years to see us on our way to, if not actually *into,* glory. Until recently, I could not imagine any American president with a sense of history openly expressing religious views that are so opposed to the spirit of the founders of the United States. Jefferson had a low opinion of religious—as opposed to ethical—Christianity, and no friendly view of the pre-Scofield Old Testament, while the non-Christian Lincoln's appeals to the

Almighty were as vague as Confucius's ritual hymns to Heaven. The American republic was created by men of the Enlightenment, who had little or no use for sky-god systems; certainly they would have regarded the Scofield-Falwell-Reagan-sky-god as a totem more suitable for dull Neanderthals than for us neo–Cro-Magnons.

But Reagan knows nothing about Jefferson, and history is not his bag. On the other hand, "I was fortunate," he told TV evangelist Jim Bakker. "I had a mother who planted a great faith in me. . . ." In his recent book *Reagan's America,* Garry Wills tells us a great deal about Nelle Reagan who "was baptized in Tampico [Illinois], as a Disciple of Christ, by total immersion . . . on Easter Sunday 1910." She was a great influence on her son, who taught Sunday School and then attended Drake University, a Disciples' college. With mounting horror, one realizes that he may not be what all of us had hoped (even prayed), a hypocrite. Until Reagan's recent misfortunes, he had not the United States, but Armageddon on his mind.

During the presidential race of 1980, Reagan told Jim Bakker of the PTL network: "We may be the generation that sees Armageddon," while a writer for the *New York Times* reported that Reagan (1980) told a Jewish group that "Israel is the only stable democracy we can rely on as a spot where Armageddon could come." Apparently, the god of Ezekiel has a thing about the necessity of stable democratic elections *prior* to sorting out the Elect just before the Bang.

Although most American right-wingers are anti-Semites, the Armageddonists need a strong Israel in order to fulfill prophecy. So TV-evangelicals, Pentagon ("Those are the *real* anti-Semites," former Austrian Chancellor Bruno Kreisky muttered in my ear last October at Frankfurt), and right-wing politicians like Richard Nixon are all dedicated supporters of Israel. Sensibly and cynically, the Israelis exploit this religious madness.

Halsell reports that in October 1983, President Reagan told an Israeli lobby leader, Tom Dine, "You know, I turn back to your ancient prophets [Dine runs a home for retired ancient prophets where you can be denounced by the prophet of your choice] in the Old Testament, and I find myself wondering if we're the generation that's going to see that come about. I don't know if you noticed any of those prophecies lately, but believe me, they certainly describe the times we're going through." This was the year that Reagan decided to alert the nation to Gog. On March 8, 1983 he declared, "They [the Soviet Union] are the focus of evil in the modem world." Later, "I believe that communism is another sad, bizarre chapter in human history *whose last pages even now are being written* [my italics]." The old Acting President seems not to mind our approaching fiery fate. But then, of course, he's been saved, as he told George Otis. So, like Falwell, he ain't gonna be here either at the end.

3

The fifteenth of February, 1987, proved to be a bright sunny day in Hell, where I had come with nine hundred worthies from several dozen countries, to listen to Satan himself, Gorbachev, who spoke thoughtfully of the absolute necessity of abolishing all nuclear weapons on the ground that the fact of their existence endangers the human race. Plainly, the Lord of the Flies has not read the Good Book. If he had, he would know that this planet is just a staging area for that glorious place in the sky where, free of abortion and contraception and communism, the chosen will swirl about in the cosmic dust, praising the Lord for all eternity. In fact, not only did Gorbachev not seem to know the Truth that Reagan adheres to (so unlike mere irksome truth-telling), he even suggested to us that this planet may be the only one that could support a human race. It would be, he said, a pity to lose everything through war or, more likely, accident. Then, to everyone's amazement, Gorbachev mentioned Chernobyl by name, breaking the first law of the TV politician: Never acknowledge failure. Since Hitler's invasion, nothing has alarmed the Russians more than Chernobyl's fallout, which is everywhere, including the village where I live in southern Italy: There is cesium 137 at the bottom of my garden. Gorbachev owned up to the whole mess, something our Acting President would never do . . . indeed has not, specifically, done.

On April 10, 1986, in order to preserve freedom for all men everywhere, the Acting President ordered a resumption of underground nuclear testing. The test's code name was Mighty Oak; the place, Nevada. Several weeks before Chernobyl, Mighty Oak came a cropper. Some sort of unanticipated explosion went wrong. When nongovernmental analysts duly noted increased radiation in the spring zephyrs, they were told by the Department of Energy that all was well. Then, on May 7, the department admitted that the level of the radioactive inert gas xenon 133 had been detected fifty miles from the site, at 550 picocuries per cubic meter. Of course things were, as always, worse in Russia. Now we learn that of our last six nuclear underground tests, three have made the atmosphere more than ever poisonous through mishap. In August 1986, Gorbachev announced a moratorium on such tests. But Reagan chooses to ignore the moratorium and stands tall.

As I stared at the stocky round-faced little man addressing us, I tried to imagine any American politician making as straightforward and intelligent an address to the likes of Trudeau and Galbraith, Milos Forman and Berio. (Needless to say the American press ignored the substance of the speech and zeroed in on the charismatic presence of one Yoko Ono.) The only direct reference that Lucifer made to the Archangel from Warner Brothers concerned something that Reagan had said to him in Geneva: If the earth were ever to be invaded by Martians, the United States and the Soviet Union would, of course, be joint allies in a common cause. Gorbachev sighed: "I told the president that it was, perhaps, premature to prepare for such an invasion but as we had a common enemy right now, nuclear weapons, why couldn't we unite to get rid of them?" But the planter of Mighty Oaks was not to be seduced. How could he be? Nearly every major politician in the United States is paid for by what is known as "the defense industry." That is why close to 90 percent of the government's income is wasted on "defense."

Ordinarily, American conservatives (known, amusingly, as liberals) would have stopped this destruction of the economy and endangerment of life itself by the radical right (known, yet another thigh slapper, as conservatives). But things began to go awry with the invention of Israel. Many American conservatives decided that, for them, Israel comes first and so they chose to make common cause with the anti-Semitic but pro-Israel Jesus Christers, who lust for rapture.

Two years ago, Irving Kristol justified this shift in a house organ of the American Jewish Committee. Kristol noted that when the Jews were new to the American scene they "found liberal opinion and liberal politicism more congenial in their attitudes, more sensitive to Jewish concerns." So they voted for the liberal paladin, Franklin D. Roosevelt and his heirs. But now, Kristol writes, "is there any point in Jews hanging on, dogmatically and hypocritically, to their opinions of yesteryear when it is a new era we are confronting?" Because of Israel, "we are constrained to take our allies where and how we find them." Finally, "If one had informed American Jews fifteen years ago that there was to be a powerful revival of Protestant fundamentalism as a political as well as religious force, they would surely have been alarmed, since they would have assumed that any such revival might tend to be anti-Semitic and anti-Israel. But the Moral Majority is neither." But, of course, the Moral Majority is deeply anti-Semitic and will always remain so because the Jews killed our Lord (proving that no good deed ever goes unpunished: Were not those first-century Jews simply fulfilling The Divine Plan?), and the Jesus Christers are pro-Israel for reasons that have nothing to do with the Jews who are—except for exactly 144,000—going to get it along with the commies, at Armageddon.

Currently, there is little open debate in the United States on any of these matters. The Soviet Union must be permanently demonized in order to keep the money flowing to the Pentagon for "defense," while Arabs are characterized as sub-human terrorists. Israel may not be criticized at all. (Ironically, the press in Israel is far more open and self-critical than ours.) We do have one token Palestinian who is allowed an occasional word in the press, Professor Edward Said, who wrote (*Guardian,* December 21, 1986): since the "1982 Israeli invasion of Lebanon . . . it was felt by the Zionist lobby that the spectacle of ruthless Israeli power on the TV screen would have to be effaced from memory, by the strategy of incriminating the media as anti-Semitic for showing these scenes at all." A wide range of Americans were then exuberantly defamed, including myself.

I wondered, as I listened to Gorbachev, if he had any notion of the forces arrayed against him in the United States. Obviously, he is aware of the Israeli lobby, but that is something that he can come to terms with: Neither the Israelis nor the Russians are interested in suicide. But the Dispensationalists are quite another matter. By accident, the producers of that one-time hit-show the United States of America picked for the part of president a star with primitive religious longings. We cannot blame them. How could they have known? They thought that he was giving all that money to defense simply to reward them for giving him the lead, which he was doing, in part; but he was also responding to Ezekiel, and the glory of the coming end.

On the other hand, Gorbachev said that because he believes in life, the nuclear arms race will end because this is the only world that we have. We applauded. He paused. Then, with perfect timing, he said, "I had expected warmer applause on that line." We gave it to him. He laughed. The speech was soon over.

I said to Norman Mailer, "I think there should be a constitutional amendment making it impossible for anyone to be president who believes in an afterlife." Mailer said, "Well, that rules me out." I was astonished and said so. "If there isn't an afterlife," he said, "then what's the point to all this?" Before I could answer, he said, "All right, all right. I know what you're going to say. There is no point." A pride of exotic bishops separated us.

Yes, that is what I would have said, and because there is no cosmic point to the life that each of us perceives on this distant bit of dust at galaxy's edge, all the more reason for us to maintain in proper balance what we have here. Because there is nothing else. No thing. This is it. And quite enough, all in all.

—*The Observer* (London)
November 15, 1987
(But written as of March 1987
In *The Nation*)

SIX

NOTES ON OUR
PATRIARCHAL STATE

Thomas Jefferson. This is where it all begins. With his Declaration of Independence, he created the idea of the American Revolution, as opposed to the less glamorous

and certainly less noble business of simply deciding who pays tax to whom. Along with the usual separated-colony boilerplate, there would be a new nation founded upon life, liberty, and the pursuit of happiness. The first two foundation stones were familiar, if vague. What, after all, is liberty? Liberty from what? From everyone else? From decent opinion? From accountability? That debate goes on. But the notion of freedom from tyranny is an ancient one, and everyone thinks he knows what Jefferson meant, including dreamy Tom himself.

The "pursuit of happiness" is the real joker in the deck. No one is quite sure just what Jefferson meant, but I suppose he had it in mind that government would leave each citizen alone to develop as best he can in a tranquil climate to achieve whatever it is that his heart desires with minimum distress to the other pursuers of happiness. This was a revolutionary concept in 1776. It still is. With a single phrase, Jefferson had upped the ante and made our Republic—in name, at least—more human-scale than any other.

Eventually we freed ourselves from England, thanks to the French fleet. At the end of the struggle, there was George Washington, and hardly anyone else except a group of ambitious lawyers, overexcited by the prospect of a new nation with new laws and a complex judiciary in need of powerful advocates and prosecutors and interpreters. Hence a most lawyerly Constitution that, in effect, excluded from citizenship women, slaves, Native Americans, and the poor. The Constitution's famous checks and balances were designed to check the man who would be king while making certain that in the balance the people at large would have no weight at all. That is why, unlike most First World countries, the United States has elections rather than politics.

The second revolutionary note was struck in 1791. Although the Founding Fathers were, to a man, natural conservatives, there were enough Jefferson-minded pursuers of happiness among them to realize that so lawyerly a Republic would probably serve as a straitjacket for those of an energetic nature. Therefore, to ensure the right of each to pursue happiness, the Bill of Rights was attached to the Constitution. In theory, henceforward no one need fear the tyranny of either the state or the majority.

Certain of our rights, such as freedom of speech, were said to be inalienable. But a significant minority has never accepted the idea of so much freedom for so many. That is why, from 1791 to the present day, the ongoing drama of our Republic has been the relentless attack of the prosperous few upon the rights of the restless many—often masked as the righteous will of the majority against the deviant few. The current Supreme Court is clearly dedicated to the removal or alienation of as many of our inalienable rights as possible, on the specious ground that what the founders did not spell out as a "right" was not a right at all, but some sort of unpatriotic, un-American activity.

The result has been confusion, to put it mildly. The Fourteenth Amendment made it clear that those freedoms guaranteed to persons as citizens of the United States also applied to them as citizens of pure Utah or sex-sickened Georgia. But, so the argument goes, if the Constitution does not say that you may smoke marijuana, then any state may forbid you to smoke what a local majority thinks is bad for you. On the other hand, if the producers of death-enhancing consumer items have enough money, they can buy congresses, courts, presidents; they can also hire a consumer spokesperson like Jesse Helms to uphold the constitutional right of those who wish to pursue happiness and profits by making and selling cigarettes, which kill a half-million or so people a year, while forbidding, at huge expense, heroin, which kills in the pathetically low four figures. That neither tobacco nor heroin is good for people is agreed by all. But should either be outlawed in the sort of society that Jefferson designed for us? Finally, do we want a free society or a patriarchal one? My question is not rhetorical.

Patriarchal. From the Latin *pater,* father. As in father knows best. A patriot, then, is someone who serves the *father*land. The notion of the father as chief of chiefs is prehistoric. From this tribal conceit derives monotheism: the idea of a single god-creator who has created at least half of *us* in *his* image.

Although religion may be freely practiced in these parts, it was deliberately excluded from the political arrangements of our Republic. Unfortunately, the zealous few are always busy trying to make the many submit to their religious laws and superstitions. In the 1950s they won a great—and illegal— victory over the Constitution when they put the phrase "In God We Trust" on the currency.

Although the notion of one god may give comfort to those in need of a daddy, it reminds the rest of us that the totalitarian society is grounded upon the concept of God the father. One paternal god, one paternal leader. Authority is absolute. And error, the Roman Catholic Church tells us, has no rights.

Each year it is discovered that when high school seniors are confronted blindly with the Bill of Rights, they neither like it nor approve it. Our society has made them into true patriots, believers in a stern patriarchy where the police have every right to arrest you for just about anything that Dad disapproves of. The tragedy of the United States, thus far in this century, is not the crack-up of an empire, which we never knew what to do with in the first place, but the collapse of the idea of the citizen as someone autonomous whose private life is not subject to orders from above. Today, hundreds of thousands of Americans are only marginally free as they undergo mandatory blood tests, urine tests, lie detector tests. Speech is theoretically free, but the true pulpit, electronic or print, is pretty much denied anyone who does not support the patriarchal state in all its misdeeds. It is no wonder that two-thirds of citizens under forty have no interest in public affairs. They know they are not participants in the governance of the country. They are, simply, administrative units.

I would put the time and place of our fall as the White House in 1950. Harry Truman and his advisers decided that it would be a good idea to keep the United States on a full wartime basis even though there was no enemy on earth who could challenge us militarily or economically. Therefore an enemy had to be invented. The dictator Stalin fit the bill. So did atheistic and *godless* communism as a rival religion. But, said a Republican senator to Truman, if you really want to waste all that money on the military, you're going to have to scare the hell out of the American people. With a lot of help from Congress and the likes of Henry Luce, Truman did just that.

Out of fairness to our inadvertent totalitarian, there was an urgent economic motive in 1950. We had made our recovery from the Depression of the 1930s only when the war put everyone to work. After the war, rather than run the terrible risk of a free economy in which General Motors would have to make something people wanted, like a car, we decided to take all the revenue—two-thirds, anyway—of the federal government and put it into armaments.

The second reason for our garrison state is obvious: profit. There is a third reason, but I don't think most people in 1950 were aware of its consequences. A state forever at war, hot or cold, is easily controlled by the few; unlike a relatively free society, in which the governors are accountable to the people at large and to law. Today the neglected, ignored people have got the point; half the electorate refuses to vote in presidential elections. After all, was there any difference between Dukakis and Bush? Admittedly, Dukakis did not seem to mind too much if Kitty was raped by black prisoners on furlough, while Bush thought the flag was just grand, even if it was made in Taiwan. This was all good fun of the kind our rulers, who gave us prime-time television, think the idiots—us—will lap up. But then it is their job to divert public attention from the great corruption of the Pentagon and S&Ls and toxic waste. In the end there was a difference between the two: Dukakis wanted to increase the Pentagon budget by $4 billion, Bush by $11 billion. This being the extent of disagreement between the parties, it is clear that neither is an instrument by which the people might assert themselves and make known their will. As for a third party, we tried that in 1972. The People's Party. Unfortunately, we hadn't realized that to have a third party, you must have two other parties. We also found out that political parties, as opposed to spontaneous movements, are not possible in an oligarchy as entrenched as the one that rules us.

The small group that pays for the presidents and the congresses maintains its grip on the country through the media and the schools. After all, if the people hadn't bought the idea that Noriega was the number-one drug dispenser, Panama could not have been illegally invaded so that Bush might not seem a wimp. Thousands of Panamanians died, as well as twenty-three American servicemen (nine of them killed by other Americans), for no purpose other than shoring up the image of the oligarchs' current spokesman, George Bush. Since the reading skills of the American people are the lowest in the First World, the general public is always easy prey to manipulation by television. This means that if you want to demonize drugs or the Arabs or the Japanese, you do so openly in the media. You also do it subliminally. As a result, in the past two years, drugs was pushed from tenth to first place as a national worry. Now that communism has ceased to be the unholy devil, drug dealers, and users, are the enemy. Aircraft carriers are needed off the coast of Colombia to intercept drug exporters. And so two-thirds of the true budget will continue to go to the government in its latest "war"—a war that will not be won because no one has any interest in winning it, as opposed to expensively prosecuting it. The oligarchy does not care whether the citizens make themselves sick with drugs or not. What government wants is simple: total control. If this can be got by dispensing with the Bill of Rights, then that's a small price to pay. The whole tone of the Reagan-Bush management is one of open hostility to our ancient rights in particular and to the people in general. Today the poor, as Mr. Bush might put it, are in deep doo-doo. The rich are fed up with the poor. And if the poor don't shape up, the rich just aren't going to take it anymore.

The problem is money: who has it, who spends it, and who gets what for what he paid. When it costs $40 million to create a presidential candidate, he is not going to show much interest in the people at large. He will represent the folks who gave him the $40 million. Example: Bush. Since his election, what has he fought for? Environment? Education? No. His one crusade has been the cutting of the capital-gains tax. That was the price the corporations demanded in exchange for buying him, rather than Dukakis, the presidency.

For thirty years I have made the same proposal to correct the great corruption. No candidate or party may buy time or space in the media. Give free media time and space to all candidates. Limit national election campaigns to four or six or eight weeks, which is, more or less, what other First World countries do. A single act of Congress could make our elections unbuyable. However, those who have been elected by the present system are not about to change it.

The two parties, which are really one party, cannot be put

to use. They are the country's ownership made carnival. Can the united action of individual citizens regain some control over the government? I think so. But it won't be easy, to riot in understatement. Attempts to cut back the war budget—whether the war be against communism or drugs or us—will be fought with great resourcefulness. When challenged with the billions of dollars wasted or stolen from the Pentagon, the establishment politician's answer is clear: Abortion is against God's law. He promptly changes the subject, the way a magician does when he catches your attention with one hand while the other picks your pocket.

Lately, though, our corporate oligarchs have become alarmed by one development in particular: the breakup of the nation-state almost everywhere. Since the nation-state, *as we know it*, is a nineteenth-century invention, I feel no sorrow at its demise. But those with orderly minds, eager to impose absolute order on others, are dismayed by the refusal of Latinos, say, to learn English, or Armenians to be Russian, or Québécois to be Canadian, and so on. I think this sudden worldwide desire for tribal identity is healthy, if only because our masters don't. Indeed, they have tried to make it impossible for us to use the word "race" for fear of being smeared by their media as racist—something they are, but their critics are often not. Yet we are all racist to the extent that any of us feels that he belongs to a tribe, whether it be one of color or religion or some sort of shared identity.

In actuality, we are now faced with two movements. One is centrifugal: a rushing away from the confines of a nation-state, like the Soviet Union, or from any such iron order, equally unnatural, like heterosexuality, which was invented as recently as 1930.* Simultaneously, there is a centripetal force at work: a coming together of autonomous units for certain shared ends. Hence, the Common Market in Europe. Under a loose sort of confederation, the benefits of a common currency and joint environmental action can be shared by a great many tribes or races that choose, willingly, to cooperate. So we see, on the one hand, a healthy flight from the center in order to retain individuality, and, on the other, a healthy coming together to make a "more perfect life" for the residents of the common planet. Should centripetal forces defeat centrifugal longings, however, then welcome to the anthill society, and to our inglorious common death on a speck of used-up celestial matter.

Our political debate—what little there is—can never speak of the future except in terms of the past. I shall, therefore, present a formula to restore the Republic by moving boldly forward into the past. I wish to invoke the spirit of Henry Clay. Thanks to our educational system, no one knows who he is, but for political purposes he can be first explained, then trotted out as a true America Firster who felt that it was the task of government to make internal improvements, to spend money on education and on the enlargement of the nation's economic plant. Clay, translated in a modern context, would have us abandon all military pretensions on the ground that we are too small and too poor a country to act as a global policeman. He would also suggest that we police ourselves first, and leave— terrible thought—Nicaragua to the Nicaraguans. Yes, Clay *could* be called an isolationist, but what's wrong with that?

---

* According to Jonathan Ned Katz in *Socialist Review* for February 1990, the word "heterosexual," still not acceptable to the O.E.D., first appeared in the *New York Times* (where else?) in 1930. Plainly a new category, outside the known sciences.

Our economic failure is making us more and more isolated from the rest of the industrialized world, anyway. We could use this quiet time to restore our economic health, to take a few hundred billion dollars from military procurement and put it into education, into finding new ways of training and utilizing the workforce, new ways of preserving or restoring earth and air and water. This does not seem to me to be too ambitious a program. Also, ideologically, it is absolutely—even sublimely—reactionary, and therefore salable.

But the highly progressive military-industrial-political complex will not easily let go. Ominously, our garrison state is now turning inward to create a police state. More than a million Americans are in prison or under constraint, the largest number, per capita, in the industrialized world. At least we are first at something. Currently there is a plan to reactivate old army camps to house drug users as well as pushers. Of course we could legalize drugs and get rid of the problem, but where's the money in that? Where's the fun? Where's the control over all the people all the time?

Any optimistic signs? Yes. More and more of the people who never vote are beginning to worry about their personal finances. They are looking for explanations. And now that the Reagan magic act is over, the majority that does not vote can be reached. Not through media, but through videocassettes. One can make a videocassette very cheaply, with a movie star who will work for nothing,* in order to explain, let us say, the ongoing S&L scandal. These cassettes can be

---

* I know that it is elitist to use a star when a real expert, who is really boring just like everybody else, is available. But on the nuclear freeze, say, Paul Newman was worth a dozen senators.

given out free all over the country, which is the only way that the people can be addressed directly, as they once were in the eighteenth century, through pamphlets by the likes of Thomas Paine. I got the cassette idea from that lovable old curmudgeon Ayatollah Khomeini, who flooded Iran with radio tapes from his place of exile in Paris. With those tapes he brought revolution to Iran and overthrew the Shah. I think we can do as well from our exile here at home. We will also have helped create that educated citizenry without which Jefferson felt life, liberty, and the pursuit of happiness not possible.

I began this discourse with Jefferson, as did the country, and I end it with his great injunction that, should all else fail, the tree of liberty must still be nourished with the blood, if necessary, of tyrants and of patriots. Have a nice millennium.

—*The Nation*
August 27/September 3, 1990

POSTSCRIPT:
THE PLEDGE OF ALLEGIANCE

Very few of the founders of the United States could properly be called religious men while their wives, excepting the vivid Abigail Adams, are not often on record. In the *Federalist Papers*—those notes that Madison, Hamilton, and Jay made during the making and the selling of the Constitution to the people—religion and God are hardly mentioned. When the Bill of Rights was added to the Constitution as ten amendments, the very first one declared that "Congress shall make no law respecting an establishment of religion." A principal objection to the King of England, whom we had freed ourselves from, was that he was the head of the Church of England, giving that organization precedence over all other religious groups to such an extent that England was obliged to fight a bloody civil war between the King's church and that of the rising classes who, by protesting the King and his church, became Protestants.

The founders of the American republic associated a state religion with hereditary one-man rule, and so to be feared. In old age, John Adams remarked, in a letter to Thomas Jefferson, how wonderful the world might have been without religion.

Next June, the current Supreme Court, reflexively deferential to the original intent of our founders (except, of course, when they are restlessly whittling away at the Bill of Rights) will have a crack at the First Amendment which has been something of an annoyance to the conservative (5 to 4) majority. Why?

Schoolchildren are required to recite the Pledge of Allegiance to the Flag, which reads: "I pledge allegiance to the Flag of the United States of America and to the Republic for which it stands, one nation, under God, indivisible, with liberty and justice for all." This invocation of God in a secular patriotic oath was found to be unconstitutional by the Ninth Circuit Court (June 26, 2002) on the grounds that "a profession that we are a nation 'under God' is identical ... to a profession that we are a nation 'under Jesus,' a nation 'under Vishnu,' a nation 'under Zeus,' or a nation 'under no God' because none of these professions can be neutral with respect to religion."

This decision was the result of an action brought by one Michael Newdow who brought it in order to protect his nine-year-old daughter from compulsory religious indoctrination. With some haste, the Supreme Court agreed to hear *Elk Grove Unified School District v. Newdow.*

It should be noted that both justices Scalia and Thomas have links with Opus Dei, a politically reactionary Catholic organization founded during Franco's fascist regime in Spain and today politically active in many countries. Newdow (a member of the California bar) found a speech that Scalia had given to the Knights of Columbus (a proselytizing Catholic organization) in Fredericksburg, Virginia, on January 12, 2003. Scalia attacked those who objected to government sponsorship of religion as "contrary to our whole tradition" and he cited a heckler in the crowd whose sign said, "Get religion out of government." Scalia advised, helpfully, "If the gentleman holding the sign would persuade all of you of that, then we could eliminate 'under God' from the Pledge of Allegiance. That could be democratically done." This passes for mordant wit in Scalia land.

As a result of the Fredericksburg exchange, Newdow got Scalia to recuse himself from the case. So the Court may yet be tied 4 to 4 which means that within the Ninth Circuit's jurisdiction "under God" would be dropped, but not in the rest of the nation. Meanwhile, the Christian Right is organizing, as is Ashcroft's Justice Department, which has no business at all in this nonfederal matter. But then no swallow may plunge to earth unremarked by the Attorney General's sharp God-loving eye. Apparently, Mr. Newdow has brought on a confrontation between the Constitution and that phantom nation where, as Ashcroft has solemnly declared, "Only Jesus is king." A group called Americans United hailed the Ninth Circuit's opinion on the ground that the original intent of the Founders was that "a wall," as Thomas Jefferson put it, must always be in place to separate state from church.

President Bush, a born-again Christian, predictably

denounced the Ninth Court's decision and though the Federal government has no standing in this matter, he would, he says, see to it that the government would "intervene and pursue an appeal" even though for half a century the Supreme Court has struck down all attempts to make religious instruction mandatory in school.

It is nicely ironic that the Pledge's "under God" and the currency's "In God We Trust" were duly blessed in 1954 by President Eisenhower: "In this way we are reaffirming the transcendence of religious faith in America's heritage and future; in this way we shall constantly strengthen those spiritual weapons which forever will be our country's most powerful resource in peace and war." In 1952, when teased by a fellow West Pointer that he would, if elected president, have to start going, for the first time, to church, Ike said grimly, "The only way they'll ever get me into a church will be feet first."

Those in favor of "under God" have made the point that the Declaration of Independence has three references to God and that it is a "sort of preamble to the Constitution"—a nice thought but not true: Jefferson was writing a specific indictment of King George the Third and of the notion that a hereditary monarch with an established church and religion could be the absolute master of a people three thousand miles away with, potentially, many gods, unlike the one by whom the king had been divinely anointed. God was on Jefferson's mind when he wrote his notification to the king that we were no longer his subjects.

Among the usual suspects that rally around the Under God movement has been that famous gambling dude Bill "Bell Fruit" Bennett who feels that "It doesn't affirm much in the way of religious particularity to say the Pledge of Allegiance."

But surely a sweeping generality is more dangerous than any particularity. By and large, our monolithic media ignored the principal part of the First Amendment while exercising their right, set forward in the last part, the freedom to uphold anti-Constitutional views without understanding just what they are doing.

When I was a "working" politician in the mid-Hudson Valley of New York State I heard hundreds of groups of school children and others recite The Pledge in unison. But it was not the same Pledge that we have been discussing. It had undergone a weird transformation. "One nation under God, indivisible" became "one nation under God, invisible. . . ." The tribute to Abraham Lincoln's concept of an undividable nation vanished as youthful pledgees changed the word while, at the end, this invisible nation would provide "Liberty and Justice for all," as the pledge is written but as recited "Liberty, Injustice for all," giving rise to the film director Norman Jewison's title for a very good movie called . . . *And Justice for All*. So here we go again.

SEVEN

THE NATIONAL SECURITY STATE

Every now and then, usually while shaving, I realize that I have lived through nearly one-third of the history of the United States, which proves not how old I

am but how young the Republic is. The American empire, which started officially in 1898 with our acquisition of the Philippines, came to a peak in the year 1945, while I was still part of that army which had won us the political and economic mastery of two hemispheres. If anyone had said to me then that the whole thing would be lost in my lifetime, I would have said it is not possible to lose so much so quickly without an atomic catastrophe, at least. But lose it we have.*

Yet, in hindsight, I can see that our ending was implicit in our beginning. When Japan surrendered, the United States was faced with a choice: Either disarm, as we had done in the past,

---

* I did not foresee in 1988 that the combination of a corrupt political family with roots in the oil and gas industry, aided by a neo-conservative radical cabal would seize political power in order to wage preemptive wars in Iraq and Afghanistan to enrich the family and its friends and impoverish the United States.

and enjoy the prosperity that comes from releasing so much wealth and energy to the private sector, or maintain ourselves on a full military basis, which would mean a tight control not only over our allies and such conquered provinces as West Germany, Italy, and Japan but over the economic—which is to say the political—lives of the American people. As Charles E. Wilson, a businessman and politician of the day, said as early as 1944, "Instead of looking to disarmament and unpreparedness as a safeguard against war, a thoroughly discredited doctrine, let us try the opposite: full preparedness according to a continuing plan."

The accidental president, Harry Truman, bought this notion. Although Truman campaigned in 1948 as an heir to Roosevelt's New Deal, he had a "continuing plan." Henry Wallace was onto it, as early as: "Yesterday, March 12, 1947, marked a turning point in American history, [for] it is not a Greek crisis that we face, it is an American crisis. Yesterday, President Truman . . . proposed, in effect, America police Russia's every border. There is no regime too reactionary for us provided it stands in Russia's expansionist past. There is no country too remote to serve as the scene of a contest which may widen until it becomes a world war." But how to impose this? The Republican leadership did not like the state to be the master of the country's economic life while, of the Democrats, only a few geopoliticians, like Dean Acheson, found thrilling the prospect of a military state, to be justified in the name of a holy war against something called communism in general and Russia in particular. The fact that the Soviet Union was no military or economic threat to us was immaterial. It must be made to appear threatening so that the continuing plan could be set in motion in order to create that

National Security State in which we have been living for the past forty years.

What is the National Security State? Well, it began, officially, with the National Security Act of 1947; it was then implemented in January 1950 when the National Security Council produced a blueprint for a new kind of country, unlike anything that the United States had ever known before. This document, known as NSC–68 for short, and declassified only in 1975, committed—and still, fitfully, commits—us to the following program: First, never negotiate, ever, with Russia. This could not last forever; but the obligatory bad faith of U.S.–U.S.S.R. meetings still serves the continuing plan. Second, develop the hydrogen bomb so that when the Russians finally develop an atomic bomb we will still not have to deal with that enemy without which the National Security State cannot exist. Third, rapidly build up conventional forces. Fourth, put through a large increase in taxes to pay for all of this. Fifth, mobilize the entire American society to fight this terrible specter of communism. Sixth, set up a strong alliance system, directed by the United States. (This became NATO.) Seventh, make the people of Russia our allies, through propaganda and CIA derring-do, in this holy adventure—hence, the justification for all sorts of secret services that are in no way responsible to the Congress that funds them, and so in violation of the old Constitution.

Needless to say, the blueprint, the continuing plan, was not discussed openly at the time. But, one by one, the major political players of the two parties came around. Senator Arthur Vandenburg, Republican, told Truman that if he really wanted all those weapons and all those high taxes to pay for them, he had better "scare the hell out of the American people." Truman obliged, with a series of speeches beginning on October 23, 1947, about the Red Menace endangering France and Italy; he also instituted loyalty oaths for federal employees; and his attorney general (December 4, 1947) published a list of dissident organizations. The climate of fear has been maintained, more or less zealously, by Truman's successors, with the brief exception of Dwight Eisenhower who, in a belated fit of conscience at the end of his presidency, warned us against the military-industrial complex that had, by then, established permanent control over the state.

The cynicism of this coup d'état was breathtaking. Officially, we were doing nothing but trying to preserve freedom for ourselves and our allies from a ruthless enemy that was everywhere, monolithic and all powerful. Actually, the real enemy were those National Security Statesmen who had so dexterously hijacked the country, establishing military conscription in peacetime, overthrowing governments that did not please them, and finally keeping all but the very rich docile and jittery by imposing income taxes that went as high as 90 percent. That is quite an achievement in a country at peace.

We can date from January 1950 the strict governmental control of our economy and the gradual erosion of our liberties, all in order to benefit the economic interest of what is never, to put it tactfully, a very large group—defense spending is money but not labor-intensive. Fortunately, all bad things must come to an end. Our huge indebtedness has made the maintenance of the empire a potential nightmare; and the day Japan stops buying our Treasury bonds, the troops and the missiles will all come home to a highly restless population.

Now that I have defined the gloomy prospect, what solutions do I have? I shall make five proposals. First, limit presidential election campaigns to eight weeks. That is what most civilized countries do, and all democratic ones are obliged to do. Allow no paid political ads. We might then entice that half of the electorate which never votes to vote.

Second, the budget: The press and the politicians constantly falsify the revenues and the disbursements of the federal government. How? By wrongly counting Social Security contributions and expenditures as part of the federal budget. Social Security is an independent, slightly profitable income-transferring trust fund, which should be factored out of federal revenue and federal spending. Why do the press and the politicians conspire to give us this distorted view of the budget? Because neither they nor their owners want the public to know how much of its tax money goes for a war that does not exist. As a result Federal Reserve chairman Alan Greenspan could say last March, and with a straight face, that there are only two options for a serious attack on the deficit. One is to raise taxes. The other is to reduce the entitlement programs like Social Security and Medicare. He did not mention the defense budget. He did not acknowledge that the so-called entitlements come from a special fund. But then, he is a disciple of Ayn Rand.

In actual fact, close to 90 percent of the disbursements of the federal government go for what is laughingly known as "defense." This is how: In 1986 the gross revenue of the government was $794 billion. Of that amount, $294 billion were Social Security contributions, which should be subtracted from the money available to the National Security State. That leaves $500 billion. Of the $500 billion, $286 billion go to defense; $12 billion for foreign arms to our client states; $8 billion to $9 billion to energy, which means, largely, nuclear weapons; $27 billion for veterans' benefits, the sad and constant reminder of the ongoing empire's recklessness; and, finally, $142 billion for interest on loans that were spent, over the past forty years, to keep the National Security State at war, hot or cold. So, of 1986's $500 billion in revenue, $475 billion was spent on National Security business. Of that amount, we will never know how much was "kicked back" through political action committees and so-called "soft money" to subsidize candidates and elections. Other federal spending, incidentally, came to $177 billion in 1986 (guarding presidential candidates, cleaning the White House), which was about the size of the deficit, since only $358 billion was collected in taxes.

It is obvious that if we are to avoid an economic collapse, defense spending must be drastically reduced. But it is hard to reduce a budget that the people are never told about. The first politician who realizes why those politicians who appear to run against the government always win, could not only win himself but be in a position to rid us of the National Security State—which is what people truly hate. "Internal Improvements" was the slogan of Henry Clay's popular movement. A neo-Clayite could sweep the country if he wanted seriously to restore the internal plant of the country, rather than invade Honduras or bob expensively about the Persian Gulf or overthrow a duly elected government in Nicaragua while running drugs (admittedly, the CIA's only margin of profit).

Third, as part of our general retrenchment, we should withdraw from NATO. Western Europe is richer and more populous than America. If it cannot defend itself from an enemy who seems to be falling apart even faster than we are, then there is nothing that we, proud invaders of Grenada, can effectively do. I would stop all military aid to the Middle East.

This would oblige the hard-liners in Israel to make peace with the Palestinians. We have supported Israel for forty years. No other minority in the history of the United States has ever extorted so much Treasury money for its Holy Land as the Israeli lobby, and it has done this by making a common cause with the National Security State. Each supports the other. I would have us cease to pay for either.

Fourth, we read each day about the horrors of drug abuse, the murder of policemen, the involvement of our own government in drug running, and so on. We are all aware that organized crime has never been richer, nor the society more demoralized. What is the solution? I would repeal every prohibition against the sale and use of drugs, because it is these prohibitions that have caused the national corruption, not to mention most of the addiction. Since the American memory has a span of about three days, I will remind you that in 1919 alcohol was prohibited in the United States. In 1933 Prohibition was repealed because not only had organized crime expanded enormously, but so had alcoholism. What did not work then does not work now. But we never learn, which is part of our national charm. Repeal would mean that there is no money for anyone in selling drugs. That's the end of the playground pusher. That's the end of organized crime, which has already diversified and is doing very nicely in banking, films, and dry cleaning. Eventually, repeal will mean the end of mass drug addiction. As there will always be alcoholics, there will always be drug addicts, but not to today's extent. It will be safe to walk the streets because the poor will not rob you to pay for their habit.

Fifth, two years ago I described how the American empire ended the day the money power shifted from New York to

Tokyo and we became, for the first time in seventy-one years, a debtor nation. Since then, we have become the largest debtor country in history. I suggested a number of things that might be done, some of which I've mentioned again. But, above all, I see our economic survival inextricably bound up with that of our neighbor in the Northern Hemisphere, the Soviet Union. Some sort of alliance must be made between us so that together we will be able to compete with Japan and, in due course, China. As the two klutzes of the north, each unable to build a car anyone wants to drive, we deserve each other. In a speech at Gorbachev's antinuclear forum in Moscow, I quoted a Japanese minister of trade who said that Japan would still be number-one in the next century. Then, tactlessly he said that the United States will be Japan's farm and Western Europe its boutique. A Russian got up and asked, "What did he say about us?" I said that they were not mentioned but, if they did not get their act together, they would end up as ski instructors. It is my impression that the Russians are eager to be Americans, but, thanks to the brainwashing of the National Security State's continuing plan, Americans have a built-in horror of the Evil Empire, which the press and the politicians have kept going for forty years. Happily, our National Security State is in the red, in more ways than one. Time for a change?

—*The Nation*
June 4, 1988

EIGHT

THE STATE OF THE UNION: 1980

Five years and two presidents ago, I presented in the pages of ESQUIRE *my own State of the Union Address, based on a chat I'd been giving in various parts of the* republic. Acting as a sort of shadow president, I used to go around giving a true—well, Heisenberg's uncertainty principle being what it is, a truer report on the state of the union than the one we are given each year by that loyal retainer of the Chase Manhattan Bank, the American president, who is called, depending on the year, Johnson, Nixon, Ford, Carter. Although the presidents now come and go with admirable speed, the bank goes on forever, constantly getting us into deeper and deeper trouble of the sort that can be set right— or wrong—only by its man in the Oval Office. One of the bank's recent capers has got the Oval One and us into a real mess. The de-Peacock-Throned King of Kings wanted to pay us a call. If we did not give refuge to the Light of the Aryans (Banksman David Rockefeller and Banksman Henry Kissinger were the tactical officers involved), the heir of Cyrus the Great would take all his money out of the bank, out of the

Treasury bonds, out of circulation in North America. Faced with a choice between the loss of money and the loss of honor and good sense, Banksman Carter chose not to lose money. As a result, there will probably be a new president come November. But whether it is this Banksman or that, Chase Manhattan will continue to be served and the republic will continue to be, in Banksman Nixon's elegant phrase, shafted.

In 1973, Banksman D. Rockefeller set up something called the Trilateral Commission in order to bring together politicians on the make (a tautology if there ever was one) and academics like Kissinger, the sort of gung-ho employee who is always eager to start a war or to improve the bank's balance sheet. Not long after the Trilateral Commission came into being, I started to chat about it on television. Although I never saw anything particularly sinister in the commission itself (has any commission ever *done* anything?), I did think it a perfect symbol of the way the United States is ruled. When Trilateral Commission member Carter was elected president after having pretended to be An Outsider, he chose his vice-president and his secretaries of state, defense, and treasury, as well as the national security adviser, from Chase Manhattan's commission. I thought this pretty bold—even bald.

To my amazement, my warnings were promptly heeded by, of all outfits, the American Right, a group of zanies who ought deeply to love the bank and all its works. Instead, they affect to fear and loathe the Trilateral Commission on the ground that it is, somehow or other, an integral part of that international monolithic atheistic godless communist conspiracy that is bent on forcing honest American yeomen to get up at dawn and walk to work for the state as abortionists and fluoride dispensers. Needless to say, although the American

right wing is a good deal stupider than the other fragile political wings that keep the republic permanently earthbound,
their confusion in this matter is baffling. The bank is very
much their America.

Although there has never been a left wing in the United
States, certain gentle conservatives like to think of themselves
as liberals, as defenders of the environment, enemies of our
dumber wars. I would think that they'd have seen in the bank's
Trilateral Commission the perfect symbol of why we fight our
dumber wars, why we destroy the environment. But not a
single gentle liberal voice has ever been raised against the
bank. I suppose this is because too many of them work for the
Bank . . . I shall now use the word Bank (capitalized, naturally)
as a kind of shorthand not just for the Chase Manhattan, but
also for the actual ownership of the United States. To quote
from my earlier State of the Union message: "Four point four
percent own most of the United States . . . This gilded class
owns twenty-seven percent of the country's real estate. Sixty
percent of all corporate stock, and so on." The Bank is the
Cosa Nostra of the 4.4 percent. The United States government
is the Cosa Nostra of the Bank.

For more than a century, our educational system has seen
to it that 95.6 percent of the population grow up to be docile
workers and consumers, paranoid taxpayers, and eager warriors in the Bank's never-ending struggle with atheistic communism. The fact that the American government gives back to
the citizen-consumer very little of the enormous revenues it
extorts from him is due to the high cost of what the Bank—
which does have a sense of fun—calls "freedom." Although
most industrial Western (as well as Eastern) European countries have national health services, the American taxpayer is

not allowed this amenity because it would be socialism, which is right next door to godless communism and free love, followed by suicide in the long white Swedish night. A major part of our country's revenue must always go to the Pentagon, which then passes the money on to those client states, industries, and members of Congress with which the Bank does business. War is profitable for the bank. Health is not.

Five years ago, incidentally, I said: "The defense budget is currently about a quarter of the national budget—$85 billion . . . [It] is now projected for the end of the decade to cost us $114 billion. This is thievery. This is Lunacy." The requested defense budget for the first year of our brand-new decade is $153.7 billion, which is still thievery, still lunacy—and highly inflationary to boot. But since the defense budget is at the heart of the Bank's system of control over the United States, it can never be seriously reduced. Or, to put it another way, cut the defense budget and the Bank will start to die.

Since my last State of the Union Address, the election law of 1971 has come into its ghastly own. The first effect of the law was to give us the four-year presidential campaign. The second treat we got from it was the presidency of Banksman Jimmy Carter. It is now plain that anyone who can get elected president under the new ground rules ought not to be allowed to take office.

For once, even the dullest of the Bank's depositors is aware that something is wrong. Certainly, there have never been quite so many demonstrably dim Banksmen running for president as there are in 1980. Part of this is historical: Not since the country's bright dawn have first-rate people gone into politics. Other countries take seriously their governance. Whatever one might think of the politics of Giscard d'Estaing and Helmut Schmidt, each is a highly intelligent man who is proud to hold a place in the government—unlike his American equivalent, who stays out of politics because the Bank fears the superior man. As a result, the contempt in which Carter is held by European and Japanese leaders is not so much the fault of what I am sure is a really swell Christian guy as it is due to the fact that he is intellectually inferior to the other leaders. The Bank prefers to keep the brightest Americans hidden away in the branch offices. The dull and docile are sent to Congress and the White House.

I don't know any thoughtful person who was not made even more thoughtful by the recent Canadian election. The new prime minister was not popular. He made mistakes. In the course of a half-hour vote of no confidence, the government fell. There was a nine-and-a-half-week campaign that cost about $60 million. At its end, the old prime minister was back. In a matter of weeks there had been a political revolution. If the United States had had a parliamentary system last April, we would have been relieved of Jimmy Carter as chief of government after his mess in the Iranian desert. But he is still with us, and the carnival of our presidential election goes on and on, costing tens of millions of dollars, while the candidates smile, shake hands, and try to avoid ethnic jokes and the demonstration of any semblance of intelligence. Although the economy is in a shambles and the empire is cracking up, the political system imposed upon us by the Bank does not allow any candidate to address himself seriously to any issue. I know that each candidate maintains, in some cases accurately, that he has superb position papers on all the great issues; but no one pays any attention—further proof that the system doesn't work. After all, since the Bank owns the media, the

Bank is able to decide who and what is newsworthy and just how much deeptalk its depositors can absorb. Plainly, the third American republic is drawing to a close and we must now design for ourselves a fourth republic, a democratic society not dedicated to war and the Bank's profits. Third republic? Fourth republic? What am I talking about? Let me explain.

The first American republic began with the revolution in 1776 and ended with the adoption of the Constitution in 1787. The first republic was a loose confederation of thirteen autonomous states who subscribed, more or less, to certain articles. The second republic was also a fairly loose affair until 1861, when the American Bismarck, Abraham Lincoln, took the mystical position that no state could ever leave the Union. When the southern states disagreed, a bloody war was fought in order to create "a more perfect *[sic]* union." At the war's end, our third and most imperial republic came into existence. This republic was rich, belligerent, hungry for empire. This republic's master was the Bank. This republic became, in 1945, the world's master. Militarily and economically, the third American republic dominated the globe. All then should have been serene: The mandate of Heaven was plainly ours. Unfortunately, the Bank made a fatal decision. To keep profits high, it decided to keep the country on a permanent wartime footing. Loyal Banksman Harry S. Truman deliberately set out to frighten the American people. He told us that the Soviet Union was on the march while homegrown Reds were under every bed—all this at a time when the United States had atomic weapons and the Russians did not, when the Soviet Union was still in pieces from World War II and we were incredibly prosperous.

Those who questioned the Bank's official line were called "commies" or "soft on communism." Needless to say, in due course, the Soviet Union did become the powerful enemy that the Bank requires in order to keep its control of the third republic. The business of our third republic is war, or defense, as it's been euphemistically called since 1949. As a result, of the thirty-five years since the end of World War II, the United States has managed to be at war (hot and cold) for thirty; and if the Bank has its way, we shall soon be at war again, this time on a really large scale. But then, as Banksman Grover Cleveland observed so presciently almost a century ago, "the United States is not a country to which peace is necessary."

There comes a time, however, when the waging of war is too dangerous even for Banksmen. There also comes a time when the crude politics of getting the people to vote against their own interests by frightening them with the Red Menace simply doesn't work. We are now in such a time. Clearly, a new sort of social arrangement is necessary.

The fact that half of those qualified to vote don't vote in presidential elections is proof that the third republic is neither credible nor truly legitimate. The fact that the Bank's inspired invention, the so-called two-party system (which is really one single Banksparty), is now irrelevant to half the electorate is further proof that the fourth republic will require political parties that actually represent the various groups and classes in the country and do not simply serve the Bank. By breaking out of the two-party system this year, Banksman John Anderson has demonstrated in the most striking way that, like the Wizard of Oz, the two-party system never really existed.

The time has come to hold another constitutional convention. Those conservatives known as liberals have always found this notion terrifying, because they are convinced that the powers of darkness will see to it that the Bill of Rights is abolished. This is always a possibility, but sometimes it's best to know the worst all at once rather than to allow those rights to be slowly taken away from us by, let us say, the present majority of the Supreme Court, led by Banksman Burger.

In the development of a new Constitution, serious attention should be paid to the Swiss political arrangement. Its cantonal system is something that might work for us.

The United States could be divided into autonomous regions: northern California, Oregon and Washington would make a fine Social Democratic society, while the combined states of Texas, Arizona, and Oklahoma could bring back slavery and the minstrel show. There ought to be something for everybody to choose from in the United States, rather than the current homogenized overcentralized state that the Bank has saddled us with. The Swiss constitution has another attractive feature: the citizens have the right to hold a referendum and rescind, if they choose, newly promulgated federal laws. No need for a Howard Jarvis to yodel in the wilderness: the Jarvis Effect would be institutionalized.

Ideally, the fourth republic should abandon the presidential system for a parliamentary one. The leader of a majority in Congress would form the government. Out of respect for the rocks at Mount Rushmore, we would retain the office of president, but the president would be a figurehead and not what he is today—a dictator who is elected by half of half the people from a very short list given them by the Banksparty.

One aspect of our present patchwork Constitution that should be not only retained but strengthened is that part of the First Amendment which says "Congress shall make no law respecting an establishment of religion, or prohibiting the free exercise thereof"—which, according to Justice Hugo Black, "means at least this: Neither can [they] force nor influence a person to go to or remain away from church against his will or force him to profess a belief or disbelief in any religion."This is clear-cut.This is noble.This has always been ignored—even in the two pre–Bank republics. Religion, particularly the Judaeo-Christian variety, is hugely favored by the federal government. For one thing, the revenues of every religion are effectively tax-exempt. Billions of dollars are taken in by the churches, temples, Scientological basements, and Moonie attics, and no tax need be paid. As a result, various fundamentalist groups spend millions of dollars propagandizing over the airwaves, conducting savage crusades against groups they don't like, mixing in politics. Now, a church has as much right as an indi-vidual to try to persuade others that its way is the right way, but not even the Bank is allowed to advertise without first doing its duty as a citizen and paying (admittedly too few) taxes.

The time has come to tax the income of the churches. After all, they are essentially moneymaking corporations that ought to pay tax at the same rate secular corporations do.* When some of the Founders proposed that church property be tax-exempt, they meant the little white church house at the corner of Elm and Main—not the $25-billion portfolio of the Roman Catholic Church, nor the even weirder money-producing shenanigans of L. Ron Hubbard, a science-fiction writer who is now the head of a wealthy "religion" called Sci-entology, or of that peculiar Korean gentleman who may or may not be an agent of Korean intelligence but who is cer-tainly the boss of a "religion" that takes in many millions of tax-free dollars a year.

* Or did, pre-Reagan.

Here are two comments *not* to be found in any American public-school book. Thomas Jefferson: "The day will come when the mystical generation of Jesus, by the Supreme Being as his father, in the womb of a virgin, will be classed with the fable of the generation of Minerva in the brain of Jupiter." John Adams (in a letter to Jefferson): "Twenty times, in the course of my late reading, have I been on the point of breaking out.'This would be the best of all possible worlds, if there was no religion in it.' "But since the Bank approves of most religions ("Slaves, obey thy masters" is an injunction it finds irresistible), superstition continues to flourish. On the other hand, if we were to tax the various denominations, a good many religions would simply wither away, on the ground that they had ceased to be profitable to their managers.

During the 1960 presidential campaign, Richard Nixon referred to John Kennedy's Catholicism six times in practically a single breath then said, piously, that he did not think religion ought to play any part in any political election—unless, maybe, *the candidate had no religion* (and Nixon shuddered ever so slightly). As the First Criminal knew only too well, religion is the most important force not only in American politics but in world politics, too. Currently, the ninth-century Imam at Qom is threatening an Islamic holy war against Satan America. Currently, the fifth-century-B.C. prime minister of Israel is claiming two parcels of real estate because an ancient text says that the Jews once lived there. Currently, the eleventh-century Polish pope is conducting a series of tours in order to increase his personal authority and to shore up a church whose past excesses caused so many to protest that a rival Protestant church came into being—and it, in turn, hates . . .

Religion is an endless and complicated matter, and no one in his right mind can help agreeing with John Adams. Unfortunately, most of the world is not in its right mind; and the Bank can take some credit for this. For years, relations were kept tense between poor American whites and poor blacks (would you let your sister marry one?), on the ground that if the two groups ever got together in a single labor union, say, they could challenge the Bank's authority. Religion is also the basis of those laws governing personal conduct that keep the prisons overcrowded with people who get drunk, take dope, gamble, have sex in a way that is not approved by the holy book of a Bronze Age nomad tribe as reinterpreted by a group of world-weary Greeks in the first centuries of the last millennium.

The thrust of our laws at the beginning of the country—and even now—is to make what these religions regard as sin secular crimes to be punished with fines and prison terms. The result? Last year the United States shelled out some $4 billion to keep 307,000 sinners locked up. Living conditions in our prisons are a famous scandal. Although the National Advisory Commission on Criminal Justice Standards and Goals declared in 1973 that "prisons should be repudiated as useless for any purpose other than locking away people who are too dangerous to be allowed at large in a free society," there are plans to build more and more prisons to brutalize more and more people who are, for the most part, harmless. In much of Scandinavia, even vicious criminals are allowed a degree of freedom to work so that they can lead useful lives, turning over a part of the money that they earn to their victims. At present, at least five American states are experimenting with a compensatory system. All agree that the new way of handling so-called property offenders is a lot cheaper than locking them up at a cost that, in New York State, runs to $26,000 a year—more than enough to send a lively lad to Harvard, where he will soon learn how to commit his crimes against property in safe and legal ways.

But since the Bank is not happy with the idea of fewer prisons, much less with the idea of fewer crimes on the books, the Bank has now come up with something called the Omnibus Crime Bill. This has been presented in the Senate by Banksman Kennedy as S. 1722 and in the House of Representatives by Banksman the Reverend Robert F. Drinan as H.R. 6233. Incidentally, Banksman Drinan will presently give up his seat in the House at the order of the Polish pope, who says that he does not want his minions in politics, which is nonsense. A neo-fascist priest sits as a deputy in the Italian Parliament, just across the Tiber from the Vatican. Father Drinan, alas, is liberal. He does not favor the Right to Life movement. On the other hand, he is a loyal Banksman—hardly a conflict of interest, since the Vatican has an account with the Bank, administered until recently by Michele Sindona, a master criminal.

The point of these two bills is as simple as the details are endlessly complex: the Bank wants more power to put in prison those people who challenge its authority. At the moment it looks as if this repressive legislation will become law, because, as Republican Senator James A. McClure has pointed out, the Omnibus Crime Bill is now "a law unto itself, a massive re-creation whose full implications are known only by its prosecutorial draftsmen (in the Justice Department)." Some features:

If, during a war, you should advise someone to evade

military service, to picket an induction center, to burn a draft card, you can go to jail for five years while paying a fine of $250,000 (no doubt lent you by the bank at 20 percent).

If, as a civilian, you speak or write against a war in such a way that military authorities think you are inciting insubordination, you can get up to ten years in prison or pay a fine of $250,000, or both. If, as a civilian, you write or speak against a war or against conditions on a military installation, and if the Bank is conducting one of its wars at the time (according to the bill—by omission—a war is not something that Congress declares anymore), you can get ten years in prison and pay the usual quarter-million-dollar fine. If the Bank is not skirmishing someplace, you can go to jail for only five years while forking out a quarter mil.

If you break a federal law and tell your friendly law enforcer that you did not break that federal law, and if he has corroboration from another friendly cop that you did, you have made a False Oral Statement to a Law Enforcement Officer, for which you can get two years in the slammer after paying the customary quarter-mil.

Anyone who refuses to testify before a grand jury, court, or congressional committee, even though he has claimed his constitutional (Fifth Amendment) right against self-incrimination, can be imprisoned if he refuses to exchange his constitutional right to remain silent for a grant of *partial* immunity from prosecution.

The Bank's deep and abiding love of prison requires that alternatives to prison not be encouraged. According to a 1978 Congressional Research Service report, this bill (then S. 1437), enacted and enforced, would add anywhere from 62.8 to 92.8 percent to our already overcrowded federal prisons. The Bank's dream, plainly, is to put all its dissident depositors either in prison or, if they're young enough, into the army, where they lose most of their civil rights.

Needless to say, the press gets it in the chops. If you're a newspaperman and you refuse to identify your sources for a story, you are Hindering Law Enforcement, for which you can get the usual five and pay the usual quarter. If you receive documentary proof that the government is breaking the law or that its officials are corrupt, you may be guilty of Defrauding the Government, and you can get the old five and pay a quarter. On the other hand, if you are a public servant who blows the whistle on government corruption or criminality, you can get only two and pay a quarter: The Bank has a certain compassion for apostate tellers.

Finally, a judge will have the right to put any person accused of any crime in prison before he has been tried, and that same judge can then deny the accused bail for any reason that appeals to him. This provision means the end of the basis of our legal system: You are innocent until you are proved guilty. According to the *Los Angeles Times*: "What is contemplated in S. 1722 is a fundamental reordering of the relationship between people and the government. . . . Under the proposed radical revisions of federal criminal law now before Congress, we would be less free and ultimately less secure." But, (at this writing) this huge, complex assault on our liberties continues to sail through Congress, guided by Banksman Kennedy and Popesman Drinan, and looks fairly certain to pass.*

---

* The bill was defeated in the fall of 1980 by the lame-duck Congress. Like Dracula, I wrote, it is sure to rise again. It did. Post-9/11 when the first half of the USA Patriot Act passed (apparently unread) and the second is actually being studied before it is passed and we surrender due process of law, etc.

Plainly, there is a panic in the boardroom of the Bank. A number of things have started to go wrong all at once. Since energy will soon be in short supply to all the world, the third republic will be particularly hard hit, because the Bank is not capable of creating alternatives to the conventional unrenewable (and so highly profitable) sources of energy, any more than the Bank was able to anticipate the current crisis of small car versus gas-guzzler, something that consumer-depositors had figured out some time ago when they demonstrated a preference for small economic models by buying foreign cars.

The empire is cracking up because the Banksmen have never had a very clear worldview. On the one hand, they are superb pragmatists. They will do business with Mao, Stalin, Franco, the Devil, if profits can be made that way. On the other hand, simultaneously, they must continue to milk this great cow of a republic; and the only way they know to get their hands on our tax dollars is to frighten us with the menace of godless communism, not easily done when you're seen to be doing business quite happily with these godless predators. The final madness occurred when Banksman Nixon went to Peking and Moscow in search of new accounts (which he got on terms unfavorable to us) while continuing to rail against those two ruthless, inexorable enemies of all that we hold dear. This sort of schizophrenia has switched off the public and made our government a source of wonder and despair to its allies.

When Banksman Nixon was audited and found wanting, the Bank itself came under scrutiny of a sort that it is not used to. Lowly consumer-depositors now speak of a national "crisis of confidence." The ordinarily docile media have even revealed a few tips of the iceberg—no, the glacier—that covers with corruption our body politic.

Now the masters of the third republic are striking back. They are loosening the CIA's leash, which had been momentarily shortened (or so they told us). They have also come up with a new charter for the FBI that is now before the Senate (S. 1612). In testimony before the Judiciary Committee, law professor emeritus T. I. Emerson of Yale was highly critical of the new powers given the FBI. "The natural tendency of any system of law enforcement," he testified, "is to formulate its doctrines, train its personnel, and utilize its machinery to support social stability and thwart social change." Among the features of the new charter that Emerson found dangerous was the right to initiate an investigation where there is a suspicion, in the agency's eyes, that a person "will engage" in illegal activity.* This means that anyone is a potential target of the FBI because anyone might somehow, someday, do something illegal. The FBI also wants access to the financial records of political associations—an invasion of political as well as personal freedom. Finally, the new charter will pretty much remove the agency from any outside scrutiny. In so doing, it will create something that our pre–Bank republics refused to countenance: a centralized national police force. Well, as that wily old fox Benjamin Franklin once hinted, sooner or later every republic becomes a tyranny.

For 169 years, from the halls of Montezuma to the shores of Tripoli, the United States was a military success, able to overlook the odd scalped general or the White House that the British so embarrassingly burned to the ground in 1814. With considerable dash, we tore a chunk of land away from Mexico (which the Mexicans are now, sensibly, filling up again); next,

---

* This doctrine of preemption has been embraced by the Bushites.

we killed several hundred thousand Filipinos (no one has ever determined just how many) in order to establish ourselves as a regnant Pacific power at the beginning of the twentieth century; but then, after we got through two world wars in fine shape, something started to go wrong. In fact, since 1945 nothing has gone right for us. The war in Korea was a draw. The war in Vietnam was a defeat. Our constant meddling in the affairs of other countries has made us not only widely hated but, rather more serious, despised. Not unlike the Soviet Union, our opposite number, we don't seem able to maintenance our helicopters properly or to gauge in advance the world's reactions to our deeds or to have sufficient intelligence to know when to make a run for it and when to stand tall. What's wrong?

Those born since World War II have been taught to believe that the CIA has always been an integral part of American life. They don't know that the agency is only thirty-three years old, that it is essentially illegal not only in its activities (overthrowing a Chilean president here, an Iranian prime minister there) but also in its charter. The Constitution requires that "a regular Statement of Account of the Receipts and Expenditures of all Public Money shall be published from time to time." The CIA does no such thing: it spends billions of dollars a year exactly as it pleases. Although forbidden by law to operate inside the United States, the CIA has spied on American citizens at home, in merry competition with numerous other intelligence agencies whose single interest is the control of the American people in the name of freedom. Most Americans have heard of the FBI and the Treasury men and the Secret Service (though few Americans have a clear idea of what they actually do or of how much money they spend).

On the other hand, hardly anyone knows about the National Security Agency, a miniature CIA run by the Defense Department. It has been estimated that in 1975, the NSA employed 20,000 civilians, used between 50,000 and 100,000 military personnel, and had a budget of $1 billion. Needless to say, the NSA is quite as illegal as the CIA—more so, in fact. The CIA was chartered, messily but officially, by Congress; but the NSA was created secretly by presidential directive in 1952, and Congress has never legalized the agency.

All good Americans want the budget balanced, and the liquidation of the CIA and the NSA would probably save anywhere from $10 billion to $20 billion a year. For those who are terrified that we won't have enough information about our relentless and godless enemy, the State Department is a most expensive piece of machinery whose principal purpose is—or was—the gathering of information about all the countries of the world. For underground, James Bond stuff, we should rely on the organization that was so useful to us when we were successful: army intelligence. Meanwhile, as a free society—the phrase no longer has much humor in it—we ought not to support tens of thousands of spies, secret agents, and dirty-tricksters, on the practical ground that a rich, lawless, and secret agency like the CIA could, with no trouble at all, take over the United States—assuming that it has not already done so.

The Bank hopes to maintain its power through the perpetuation of that garrison state it devised for us after World War II. This can be done only by involving the country in a series of small wars that will keep tax money flowing from the citizens to the Treasury to the Pentagon to the secret agencies and, eventually, to the Bank. Meanwhile, to stifle criticism, the

Bank has ordered an all-out attack on the civil liberties of the people. There is little doubt that, from Banksman Kennedy to Banksman Thurmond, the entire political spectrum in the United States (which is always a single shade of green, just like the money) will work to take away as many of our traditional freedoms as it can. Happily, the Bank's marvelous incompetence, which gave us Nixon and Carter and is now offering (at this writing) Reagan or Bush "Versus" Carter or Kennedy, is of a kind that is bound to fail. For one thing, everyone knows that small wars have a way of escalating; and though Banksmen Nixon and Bush view with what looks like equanimity World War III, the rest of the world—including, with luck, an aroused American citizenry—may call a halt to these mindless adventures for private profit. Finally, Anderson's candidacy *could* pull the plug on the two-party-system-that-is-really-one-party apparatus that has kept the Bank in power since the 1870s.*

Meanwhile, a new constitutional convention is in order. The rights guaranteed by the Founders in the old Constitution should be reinforced; the presidential form of government should be exchanged for a more democratic parliamentary system; the secret agencies should be abolished; the revenues of the country should go to create jobs, educational and health systems, alternative forms of energy, and so on. All those things, in fact, that the Bank says we can never afford. But I am sure that what countries less rich than ours can do, we can do.

Where will the money come from? Abolish the secret

---

* "I believe in the two-party system," said Mr. Anderson in the course of his campaign, nicely pulling the plug on himself.

agencies, and gain at least $20 billion a year. Cut the defense budget by a third, and gain perhaps $50 billion. Tax the thousand and one religions, and get untold billions more. Before you know it, the chief financial support of a government become gross and tyrannous will no longer be the individual taxpayer, that perennial patsy, but the Bank, whose entry into receivership will be the aim of the fourth, the good, the democratic republic that we must start to create sometime between now and 1984.

—*Esquire*
August 1980

NINE

THE SECOND
AMERICAN REVOLUTION

*Future generations, if there are any, will date the second
American Revolution, if there is one, from the passage
of California's Proposition 13 in 1978, which obliged*
the managers of that gilded state to reduce the tax on real
estate by more than half. Historically, this revolt was not unlike
the Boston Tea Party, which set in train those events that led
to the separation of England's thirteen American colonies
from the crown and to the creation, in 1787, of the First Constitution. And in 1865 of the Second Constitution, the result
of those radical alterations made by the Thirteenth, Fourteenth, and Fifteenth amendments. Thus far we have had two
Constitutions for two quite different republics. Now a Third
Constitution—and republic—is ready to be born.

The people of the United States (hereinafter known forever and eternally as We) are deeply displeased with their government as it now malfunctions. Romantics who don't read
much think that all will be well if we would only return,
somehow, to the original Constitution, to the ideals of the
founders, to a strict construction of what the Framers (nice

word) of the First Constitution saw fit to commit to parchment during the hot summer of 1787 at Philadelphia. Realists think that an odd amendment or two and better men in government (particularly in the Oval Office, where too many round and square pegs have, in recent years, rattled about) would put things right.

It is taken for granted by both romantics and realists that the United States is the greatest country on earth as well as in the history of the world, with a government that is the envy of the lesser breeds just as the lifestyle of its citizens is regarded with a grinding of teeth by the huddled masses of old Europe—while Africa, mainland Asia, South America are not even in the running. Actually, none of the hundred or so new countries that have been organized since World War II has imitated our form of government—though, to a nation, the local dictator likes to style himself the president. As for being the greatest nation on earth, the United States's unquestioned hegemony of the known world lasted exactly five years: 1945–1950. As for being envied by the less fortunate (in a *Los Angeles Times* poll of October 1, 1980, 71 percent of the gilded state's citizens thought that the United States had "the highest living standard in the world today"), the United States has fallen to ninth place in per-capita income while living standards are higher for the average citizen in more than eight countries.

Although this sort of information is kept from the 71 percent, they still are very much aware of inflation, high taxes, and unemployment. Because they know that something is wrong, Proposition 13, once a mere gleam in the eye of Howard K. Jarvis, is now the law in California and something like it has just been enacted in Massachusetts and Arkansas.

Our ancestors did not like paying taxes on their tea; we do not like paying taxes on our houses, traditionally, the only form of capital that the average middle-class American is allowed to accumulate.

Today, thanks to the efforts of the National Taxpayers Union, thirty state legislatures have voted in favor of holding a new constitutional convention whose principal object would be to stop the federal government's systematic wrecking of the economic base of the country by requiring, somewhat naïvely, a balanced federal budget and, less naïvely, a limitation on the federal government's power to print money in order to cover over-appropriations that require over-borrowing, a process (when combined with a fifteen-year decline in industrial productivity) that has led to double-digit inflation in a world made more than usually dangerous by the ongoing chaos in the Middle East from which the West's oil flows—or does not flow.

Even the newspapers that belong to the governing establishment of the republic are beginning to fret about that national malaise which used to trouble the thirty-ninth Oval One. Two years ago, the *New York Times* printed three articles, more in sorrow than in anger, on how, why, where, when did it all go wrong? The United States is becoming increasingly difficult to govern," the *Times* keened, "because of a fragmented, inefficient system of authority and procedures that has developed over the last decade and now appears to be gaining strength and impact, according to political leaders, scholars and public interest groups across the country."

Were this not an observation by an establishment newspaper, one would think it a call for a Mussolini: "difficult to govern . . . inefficient system of authority . . ." Surely, We the

People govern, don't we? This sort of dumb sentiment is passed over by the *Times,* which notes that "the national political parties have continued to decline until they are little more than frameworks for nominating candidates and organizing Congress and some state legislatures." But this is all that our political parties have ever done (honorable exceptions are the first years of the Republican party and the non-years of the Populists). The Framers did not want political parties—or "factions," to use their word. So what has evolved over the years are two pieces of electoral machinery devoted to the acquiring of office—and money. Since neither party represents anything but the interests of those who own and administer the country, there is not apt to be much "choice" in any election.

Normally, the *New York Times* is perfectly happy with any arrangement of which the *Times* is an integral part. But a series of crazy military adventures combined with breathtaking mismanagement of the economy (not to mention highly noticeable all-out corruption among the politicos) has thrown into bright relief the failure of the American political system. So the thirty-ninth Oval One blames the people while the people blame the lousy politicians and wish that Frank Capra would once more pick up the megaphone and find us another Gary Cooper (not the second lead) and restore The Dream.

Serious establishment types worry about the Fragmentation of Power. "Our political system has become dominated by special interests," said one to the *Times,* stars falling from its eyes like crocodile tears. After all, our political system is—and was—the invention of those special interests. The government has been from the beginning the *cosa nostra* of the few and the people at large have always been excluded from the exercise of power. None of our rulers wants to change this state of affairs. Yet the heirs of the Framers are getting jittery and sense that something is going wrong somewhere. But since nothing can ever be their fault, it must be the fault of a permissive idle electorate grown fat, literally, before our eyes, which are television. So give the drones less wages; more taxes; and put them on diets.

But the politician must proceed warily; if he does not, that 71 percent which has been conned into thinking that they enjoy the world's highest standard of living might get suspicious. So for a while the operative word was "malaise" in political circles; and no effort was made to change anything. Certainly no one has recognized that the principal source of all our problems is the Second Constitution, which allows the big property owners to govern pretty much as they please, without accountability to the people or to anyone else since, for at least a century, the Supreme Court was perhaps the most active—even reckless—part of the federal machinery, as we shall now demonstrate.

There is more than the usual amount of irony in the fact that our peculiar Constitution is now under siege from those who would like to make it either more oppressive (the Right-to-Lifers who want the Constitution to forbid abortion) or from those sly folks who want to make more and more money out of their real estate shelters. But no matter what the motive for change, change is now very much in the air; and that is a good thing.

This autumn, the counsel to the president, Mr. Lloyd N. Cutler, proposed some basic changes to the Constitution.* Although Mr. Cutler's approach was tentative and highly timid

★ *Foreign Affairs,* Fall 1980.

(he found no fault at all with the Supreme Court—because he is a partner in a Washington law firm?), he does think that it is impossible for a president to govern under the present Constitution because the separation of powers has made for a stalemate between executive and legislative branches. Since "we are not about to revise our own Constitution so as to incorporate a true parliamentary system," he proceeded to make a number of suggestions that would indeed give us a quasi-parliamentary form of government—president, vice president, and representative from each congressional district would all be elected at the same time for a four-year term (Rep. Jonathan Bingham has such a bill before the house); half the Cabinet to be selected from Congress where they would continue to sit—and answer questions as in England; the president would have the power, once in his term, to dissolve the Congress and hold new elections—and the Congress would have the power, by a two-thirds vote, to call for a new presidential election; et cetera. Mr. Cutler throws out a number of other notions that would involve, at most, amendments to the Constitution; he believes that a new constitutional convention is a "non-starter" and so whatever change that is made must originate in the government as it now is even though, historically, no government has ever voluntarily dissolved itself.

Mr. Cutler also suffers from the malaise syndrome, contracted no doubt while serving in the Carter White House: "The public—and the press—still expect the President to govern. But the President cannot achieve his overall program and the public cannot fairly blame the President because he does not have the power to legislate and execute his program." This is perfect establishment nonsense. The president and the Congress together or the president by himself or the Supreme

Court on its own very special power trip can do virtually anything that they want to do as a result of a series of usurpations of powers that have been taking place ever since Chief Justice John Marshall's *Dartmouth College v. Woodward* transformed corporations into highly sensitive human beings with all Fourteenth Amendment rights.

When a president claims that he is blocked by Congress or Court, this usually means that he does not want to take a stand that might lose him an election. He will then complain that he is stymied by Congress or Court. In 1977, Carter could have had an energy policy *if* he had wanted one. What the president cannot get directly from Congress (very little if he knows how to manage those princes of corruption), he can often obtain through executive order, secure in the knowledge that the House of Representatives is not apt to exercise its prerogative of refusing to fund the executive branch: after all, it was nearly a decade before Congress turned off the money for the Vietnam War. In recent years, the presidents have nicely put Congress over a barrel through the impounding of money appropriated for projects displeasing to the executive. Impounded funds combined with the always vast Pentagon budget and the secret revenues of the CIA give any president a plump cushion on which to rest his Pharaonic crook and flail.

Obviously, a president who does not respect the decent opinion of mankind (namely, the *New York Times*) can find himself blocked by the Court and impeached by Congress. But the Nixon misadventure simply demonstrated to what extremes a president may go before his money is turned off— before the gates of Lewisberg Federal Penitentiary, like those to Hell or Disneyland, swing open.

Carter could have given us gas rationing, disciplined the oil cartels, encouraged the development of alternative forms of energy. He did none of those things because he might have hurt his chances of reelection. So he blamed Congress for preventing him from doing what he did not want to do. This is a game that all presidents play—and Congress, too. Whenever the Supreme Court strikes down a popular law which Congress has been obliged to enact against its better judgment, the Supreme Court gets the blame for doing what the Congress wanted to do but dared not. Today separation of powers is a useful device whereby any sin of omission or commission can be shifted from one branch of government to another. It is naïve of Mr. Cutler to think that the president he worked for could not have carried out almost any program *if he had wanted to*. After all, for eight years Johnson and Nixon prosecuted the longest and least popular war in American history by executive order. Congress's sacred and exclusive right to declare war was ignored (by Congress as well as by the presidents) while the Supreme Court serenely fiddled as Southeast Asia burned. Incidentally, it is startling to note that neither Congress nor the Court has questioned the *principle* of executive order, even in the famous steel seizure case.

What *was* the original Constitution all about? I mean by this, what was in the document of 1787 as defended in the *Federalist Papers* of 1787–1788 by Madison, Hamilton, and Jay. Currently, Ferdinand Lundberg's *Cracks in the Constitution* is as good a case history of that Constitution (and its two successors) as we are apt to get this troubled season. Lundberg is the latest—if not the last—in the great line of muckrakers (TR's contemptuous phrase for those who could clean with Heraclean zeal the national stables which he, among others, had soiled) that began with Steffens and Tarbell. Luckily for us, Lundberg is still going strong.

The father of the country was the father if not of the Constitution of the convention that met in May 1787, in Philadelphia. Washington had been troubled by the civil disorders in Massachusetts in particular and by the general weakness of the original Articles of Confederation in general. From Mount Vernon came the word; and it was heard—and obeyed—all around the states. Quick to respond was Washington's wartime aide Alexander Hamilton, who knew exactly what was needed in the way of a government. Hamilton arrived at Philadelphia with a scheme for a president and a senate and a supreme court to serve for life—while the state governors would be appointed by the federal government.

Although neither John Adams nor John Jay was present in the flesh at Philadelphia, Jay's handiwork, the constitution of New York State (written with Gouverneur Morris and R. J. Livingston), was on view as was that of John Adams, who wrote nearly all of the Massachusetts state constitution; these two charters along with that of Maryland were the basis of the convention's final draft, a curious document which in its separation of powers seemed to fulfill not only Montesquieu's cloudy theories of separation of powers but, more precisely, was a mirror image of the British tripartite arrangement of crown, bicameral legislature, and independent judiciary. Only the aged Franklin opted for a unicameral legislature. But the other Framers had a passion for England's House of Lords, and so gave us the Senate.

Lundberg discusses at some length just who the Framers were and where they came from and how much money they had. The state legislatures accredited seventy-four men to the convention. Fifty-five showed up that summer. About half drifted away. Finally, "no more than five men provided most of the discussion with some seven more playing fitful supporting roles." Thirty-three Framers were lawyers (already the blight had set in); forty-four were present or past members of Congress; twenty-one were rated rich to very rich— Washington and the banker Robert Morris (soon to go to jail where Washington would visit him) were the richest; "another thirteen were affluent to very affluent"; nineteen were slave owners; twenty-five had been to college (among those who had *not* matriculated were Washington, Hamilton, Robert Morris, George Mason—Hamilton was a Columbia dropout). Twenty-seven had been officers in the war; one was a twice-born Christian—the others tended to deism, an eighteenth-century euphemism for agnosticism or atheism.

All in all, Lundberg regards the Framers as "a gathering of routine politicians, eyes open for the main chance of a purely material nature. . . . What makes them different from latter-day politicians is that in an age of few distractions, many—at least twenty—were readers to varying extents in law, government, history, and classics."

Lundberg does not accept the traditional American view that a consortium of intellectual giants met at Philadelphia in order to answer once and for all the vexing questions of how men are to be governed. Certainly, a reading of the *Federalist Papers* bears out Lundberg. Although writers about the Constitution like to mention Locke, Hume, Montesquieu, and the other great savants of the Enlightenment as godfathers to the new nation, Montesquieu is quoted only four times in the *Federalist Papers*; while Hume is quoted just once (by Hamilton) in a passage of ringing banality. Locke is not mentioned. Fans of the Framers can argue that the spirit of Locke is ever-present; but then non-fans can argue that the prevailing spirit of the debate is that of the never-mentioned but always-felt Hobbes. There is one reference each to Grotius, Plato, and Polybius. There are three references to Plutarch (who wrote about great men) and three to Blackstone (who showed the way to greatness—or at least the higher solvency—to lawyers). God is mentioned (in the Thank God sense) by Madison, a clergyman's son who had studied theology. Jesus, the Old and New Testaments, abortion, and women's rights are not alluded to. The general tone is that of a meeting of the trust department of Sullivan and Cromwell.

Lundberg quotes Merrill Jensen as saying, "Far more research is needed before we can know, if ever, how many men actually voted for delegates to the state conventions [which chose the Framers]. An old guess that about 160,000 voted—that is, not more than one-fourth or one-fifth of the total adult (white) male population—is probably as good as any. About 100,000 of these men voted for supporters of the Constitution and about 60,000 for its opponents." It should be noted that the total population of the United States in 1787 was about 3,000,000, of which some 600,000 were black slaves. For census purposes, each slave would be counted as three-fifths of a person within the First Republic.

The Framers feared monarchy and democracy. In order to prevent the man who would be king from assuming dictatorial powers and the people at large from seriously affecting the business of government, the Framers devised a series of checks and balances within a tripartite government that would, they hoped (none was very optimistic: they were practical men), keep the people and their passions away from government and the would-be dictator hedged 'round with prohibitions.

In the convention debates, Hamilton took on the romantic notion of the People: "The voice of the people has been said to be the voice of God; and however generally this maxim has been quoted and believed, it is not true in fact. The people are turbulent and changing; they seldom judge or determine right. Give therefore to [the rich and wellborn] a distinct, permanent share in the government." The practical old Tory Gouverneur Morris took the same view, though he expressed himself rather more serenely than the fierce young man on the make: "The rich will strive to establish their dominion and enslave the rest. They always did. They always will. The proper security against them is to form them into a separate interest." Each was arguing for a Senate of lifetime appointees, to be chosen by the state legislatures from the best and the richest. It is curious that neither envisioned political parties as the more natural way of balancing economic interests.

Since Hamilton's dark view of the human estate was shared rather more than less by the Framers ("Give all the power to the many, they will oppress the few. Give all power to the few, they will oppress the many"), the House of Representatives was intended to be the principal engine of the tripartite government. Like the British Parliament, the House was given (in Hamilton's words) "The exclusive privilege of originating money bills. . . . The same house will possess the sole right of instituting impeachments; the same house will be the umpire in all elections of the President. . . ." And Hamilton's ultimate defense of the new Constitution (*Federalist Paper* No. 60) rested on the ingenious way that the two houses of Congress and the presidency were chosen: "The House of Representatives . . . elected immediately by the people, the Senate by the State legislatures, the President by electors chosen for that purpose by the people, there would be little probability of a common interest to cement these different branches in a predilection for any particular class of electors."

This was disingenuous: The electoral franchise was already so limited in the various states that only the propertied few had a hand in electing the House of Representatives and the state legislatures. Nevertheless, this peculiar system of government was a success in that neither the mob nor the dictator could, legally at least, prevail. The turbulent "democratic" House would always be reined in by the appointed senators in combination with the indirectly elected president and his veto. The Constitution gave the oligarch, to use Madison's word, full possession of the government—the object of the exercise at Philadelphia. Property would be defended, as George Washington had insisted that it should be. Since Jefferson's teeth were set on edge by the word "property," the euphemism "pursuit of happiness" had been substituted in the Declaration of Independence. Much pleased with this happy phrase, Jefferson recommended it highly to the Marquis de Lafayette when he was Rights of Man-ing it in France.

The wisest and shrewdest analysis of how the House of Representatives would evolve was not provided by the would-be aristo Hamilton but by the demure James Madison. In *Federalist Paper* No. 59, Madison tried to set at ease those who feared that popular gathering in whose horny hands had been placed the national purse. Madison allowed that as the nation increased its population, the House would increase its membership. But, said he with perfect candor and a degree of complacency,

The people can never err more than in supposing that by multiplying their representatives beyond a certain limit they strengthen the barrier against the government of the few. Experience will forever admonish them that . . . they will counteract their own views by every addition to their representatives. The countenance of the government may become more democratic, but the soul that animates it will be more oligarchic [because] the greater the number composing [a legislative assembly] the fewer will be the men who will in fact direct their proceedings.

Until the present—and temporary—breakdown of the so-called lower House, this has proved to be the case.

By May 29, 1790, the Constitution had been ratified by all the states. The need for a bill of rights had been discussed at the end of the convention, but nothing had been done. Rather than call a second convention, the Bill of Rights was proposed—and accepted—as ten amendments to the new Constitution. A principal mover for the Bill of Rights was George Mason of Virginia, who had said, just before he left Philadelphia, "This government will set out [commence] a moderate aristocracy: it is at present impossible to foresee whether it will, in its operation, produce a monarchy, or a corrupt, tyrannical [oppressive] aristocracy: it will most probably vibrate some years between the two, and then terminate in one or the other." The words in brackets were supplied by fellow Virginian—and notetaker—Madison. As the ancient Franklin observed brightly, sooner or later every republic becomes a tyranny. They liked reading history, the Framers.

But the wild card in the federal apparatus proved not to be the predictable Congress and the equally predictable presidency whose twistings and turnings any reader of

Plutarch might have anticipated. The wild card was the Supreme Court.

Lundberg calls attention to the following language of Article III of the Constitution:

> "The Supreme Court shall have appellate jurisdiction, both as to law and fact, *with such exceptions, and under such regulations as the Congress shall make.*"
>
> The preceding twelve words [he continues] are emphasized because they are rarely alluded to in discussions about the Court. They bring out that, under the Constitution, the Supreme Court is subject to regulation by Congress, which may make exceptions among the types of cases heard individually or by categories. *Congress, in short, is explicitly empowered by the Constitution to regulate the Court,* not *vice versa.*

Certainly, the Court was never explicitly given the power to review acts of Congress. But all things evolve, and it is the nature of every organism to expand and extend itself.

In 1800, the outgoing Federalist President John Adams made a last-minute appointment to office of one William Marbury. The incoming Republican President Jefferson ordered his Secretary of State Madison to deny Marbury that office. Marbury based his right to office on Section 13 of Congress's Judiciary Act of 1789. Federalist Chief Justice John Marshall responded with marvelous cunning. In 1803 *(Marbury v. Madison)* he found unconstitutional Section 13, the work of Congress; therefore, the Court was unable to go forward and hear the case. The partisan Marshall must have been secretly ecstatic: he had set a precedent. In passing, as it were, Marshall had established the right of the Supreme Court to review acts of Congress.

The notion of judicial review of the Executive or of Congress was not entirely novel. Hamilton had brought up the matter in 1787 (*Federalist Paper* No. 78). "In a monarchy [the judiciary] is an excellent barrier to the encroachments and representations of the representative body." But the other Framers did not accept, finally, Hamilton's view of the Court as a disinterested umpire with veto power over the legislative branch. Yet Hamilton had made his case most persuasively; and he has been much echoed by subsequent upholders of judicial review.

Hamilton believed that the judiciary could never be tyrannous because it lacked real power; he does admit that "some perplexity respecting the rights of the courts to pronounce legislative acts void because contrary to the Constitution, has arisen from an imagination that the doctrine would imply a superiority of the judiciary to the legislative power. It is urged that the authority which can declare the acts of another void must necessarily be superior to the one whose acts must be declared void." Since this is true and since the Constitution that Hamilton is defending does *not* give judicial review to the Supreme Court, Hamilton does a most interesting dance about the subject. The Constitution is the "fundamental law" and derives from the people. If the legislative branch does something unconstitutional it acts against the people and so a disinterested court must protect the people from their own Congress and declare the act void.

Nor does this conclusion by any means suppose a superiority of the judicial to the legislative power. It only supposes that the power of the people is superior to both, and that where the will of the legislature, declared in its statutes, stands in opposition to that of the people, declared in the Constitution, the judges ought to be governed by the latter rather than the former.

This is breathtaking, even for Hamilton. He has now asserted that a court of life appointees (chosen from the rich and wellborn) is more interested in the rights of the people than the House of Representatives, the only more or less democratically elected branch of the government. But Hamilton is speaking with the tongue of a prophet who knows which god he serves. The future in this, as in so much else, was what Hamilton had envisaged, constitutional or not. Characteristically, by 1802, he had dismissed the Constitution as "a frail and worthless fabric."

Marshall was most sensitive to the charge of judicial usurpation of congressional primacy; and during the rest of his long tenure on the bench, he never again found an act of Congress unconstitutional. But Marshall was not finished with republic-shaping. Although he shared the Framers' passion for the rights of property, he did not share the admittedly subdued passion of certain Framers for the rights of the citizens. In 1833, Marshall proclaimed (speaking for a majority of his Court in *Barron v. City of Baltimore*) that the Bill of Rights was binding only upon the federal government and not upon the states. In order to pull off this caper, Marshall was obliged to separate the amendments from the Constitution proper so that he could then turn to Article VI, Paragraph 2, where it is written that this Constitution (pre–Bill of Rights) "shall be the supreme law of the land . . . any thing in the Constitution or laws of any state to the contrary not withstanding." Apparently, the first ten amendments were not an integral part of "this Constitution."

The result of Marshall's decision was more than a century of arbitrary harassment of individuals by sheriffs, local police, municipal and state governing bodies—to none of whom the Bill of Rights was held to apply. As for the federal government, the Supreme Court was only rarely and feebly willing to enforce the rights of citizens against it. It is startling to think that the Supreme Court did not seriously begin to apply the Bill of Rights to the states until the 1930s despite the Fourteenth Amendment (1868), which had spelled out the rights of citizens. Gradually, over the last thirty years, an often grudging court has doled out to the people of the United States (including Mr. Brown) most of those rights which George Mason had wanted them to have in 1793.

Fifty-four years after *Marbury v. Madison,* the Supreme Court found a second act of Congress unconstitutional. In order to return property to its owner (the slave Dred Scott to his master, Dr. Emerson), the Supreme Court declared unconstitutional the Missouri Compromise; and made inevitable the Civil War. It was ironic that the Court which Hamilton had proposed so Jesuitically as a defender of the people against a wicked legislature should, in its anxiety to protect property of any kind, have blundered onto a stage where it had neither competence nor even provenance. (Article IV: "The Congress shall have power to dispose of and make all needful rules and regulations respecting the territory or other property belonging to the United States . . .") But the wild card had now been played. Judicial review was a fact. The Court was now ready—give or take a Civil War or two—to come into its unconstitutional own.

In 1864, the Court struck down the income tax, denying Congress its absolute power to raise revenue; and not until the passage of the Sixteenth Amendment (1913) did Congress get back its right, in this instance, to raise taxes—which it can never *not* have had, under the Constitution. But as Lundberg says, "The Court had gained nearly eighteen years of tax-free bliss for its patrons although it was shown to be out of harmony with the thinking of the country as well as that of the framers, previous courts, and legal scholars—and the Constitution."

From March 9, 1865 (when the management of the reigning Republican party became almost totally corrupt), to 1970, ninety acts of Congress were held void in whole or in part. Most of these decisions involved property and favored large property owners. As of 1970, the Court had also managed to overrule itself 143 times. Plainly, the Constitution that the justices keep interpreting and reinterpreting is a more protean document than the Framers suspected. "The trouble with the Constitution of the United States," wrote the *London Chronicle* a century ago, "is that nobody has ever been able to find out what it means." Or, put another way, since everybody knows what it means, much trouble must be taken to distort the meaning in order to make new arrangements for the protection of property.

Lundberg takes the position that, by and large, the Court's behavior is the result of a tacit consensus among the country's rulers: that 2 percent of the population—or 1 percent, or sixty families, or those *active* members of the Bohemian Club owns most of the wealth of a country that is governed by the rulers' clients in the three branches of government. On those occasions when their Congress is forced by public opinion to pass laws that they do not want enacted, like the income tax of 1864, they can count either on their president's veto or on the Court's invocation of the Constitution to get Congress off the hook. The various courts are so devised, Lundberg writes, as to "rescue the legislatures and executives from their own reluctant acts."

Except for the passing of the Sixteenth Amendment, Congress has made only two serious attempts to reclaim its constitutional primacy over the Court (as opposed to a lot of unserious attempts). The first was in 1868. The House Judiciary Committee, fearful that the Court would strike down a number of Reconstruction acts, reported a bill requiring that two-thirds of a court's judges must concur in any opinion adverse to the law. This bill passed the House but died in the Senate. In the same year, the House did manage to pass a law (over presidential veto) to limit certain of the Court's appellate powers. On March 19, 1869, the Court unanimously bowed to Congress, with a sideswipe to the effect that although the Constitution did vest them with appellate powers, the clause that their powers were conferred "with such exceptions and under such Regulations as Congress shall make" must be honored.

This is one of the few times that Congress has asserted directly its constitutional primacy over a Court that for the next seventy years took upon itself more and more the powers not only to review any and all acts of Congress but to make law itself, particularly when it came to preventing the regulation of corporations or denying rights to blacks. During the last forty years, although the Court has tended to stand aside on most economic matters and to intervene on racial ones, the Court's record of self-aggrandizement has been equaled only by that of the Johnny-come-lately wild card, the president.

The first fifteen presidents adjusted themselves to their roomy constitutional cage and except for an occasional rattling of the bars (the Alien and Sedition Acts) and one breakout (the Louisiana Purchase) they were fairly docile prisoners of Article II. In 1860, the election of the sixteenth president caused the Union to collapse. By the time that Abraham Lincoln took office, the southern states had organized themselves into what they called a confederacy, in imitation of the original pre–Constitution republic. As Lincoln himself had declared in 1847, any state has the moral and, implicitly, constitutional right to govern itself. But permissive Congressman Lincoln was not stern President Lincoln. Firmly he put to one side the Constitution. On his own authority, he levied troops and made war; took unappropriated money form the Treasury; suspended habeas corpus. When the aged Chief Justice Taney hurled the Constitution at Lincoln's head, the president ducked and said that, maybe, all things considered, Congress ought now to authorize him to do what he had already done, which Congress did.

Lincoln's constitutional defense for what he had done rested upon the oath that he had sworn to "preserve, protect and defend the Constitution" as well as to see to it "that the law be faithfully executed." Lincoln proved to be a satisfactory dictator, and the Union was preserved. But the balances within the constitution of the Republic had been forever altered. With the adoption of the Thirteenth, Fourteenth, and Fifteenth Amendments extending the vote to blacks (and, by

1920, to women and, by 1970, to eighteen- to twenty-year-olds) while ensuring, yet again, that no state can "deprive any person of life, liberty, or property without due process of law; nor deny to any person within its jurisdiction the equal protection of the laws," the Bill of Rights was at last, officially at least, largely applicable to the people who lived in the states that were again united.

Needless to say, the Supreme Court, often witty if seldom wise, promptly interpreted the word "person" to mean not only a human being but a corporate entity as well. During the next fifty years, the Court continued to serve the propertied interests against any attack from the other branches of government while ignoring, as much as possible, the rights of actual persons. Any state that tried to curb through law the excesses of any corporation was sure to be reminded by the Court that it had no such right.

But the Second Republic had been born; the electorate had been expanded; and civil rights were on the books if not engraved in letters of fire upon the hearts of the judiciary. Although the presidents pretty much confined themselves to their constitutional duties, the memory of Lincoln was—and is—a constant stimulus to the ambitious chief magistrate who knows that once the nation is at war his powers are truly unlimited, while the possibilities of personal glory are immeasurable.*

At the turn of the century Theodore Roosevelt nicely arranged a war for his president, McKinley, who did not particularly want one. In 1917 Wilson arranged a war which neither Congress nor nation wanted. Since then the presidents

---

* Written long before Bush declared himself a "wartime president."

have found foreign wars irresistible. With the surrender of Japan in 1945, the last official war ended. But the undeclared wars—or "police actions"—now began with a vengeance, and our presidents are very much on the march. Through secret organizations like the CIA, they subvert foreign governments, organize invasions of countries they do not like, kill or try to kill foreign leaders while spying, illegally, on American citizens. The presidents have fought two major wars—in Korea and Vietnam—without any declaration of war on the part of Congress.

Finally, halfway through the executive's war in Vietnam, the sluggish venal Congress became alarmed—not to mention hurt—at the way they had been disregarded by Johnson Augustus. The Senate Committee on Foreign Relations began to ask such questions as, by what inherent right does a president make war whenever he chooses? On March 8, 1966, the president (through a State Department memorandum) explained the facts of life to Congress: "since the Constitution was adopted there have been at least 125 instances in which the President has ordered the armed forces to take action or maintain positions abroad without obtaining prior Congressional authorization, starting with the 'undeclared war' with France (1798–1800). . . ." Congress surrendered as they had earlier when the inexorable Johnson used a murky happening in the Tonkin Bay to ensure their compliance to his war. It was not until many thousands of deaths later that Congress voted to stop funds for bombing the Indochinese.

How did the president break out of his cage? The bars were loosened by Lincoln, and the jimmy that he used was the presidential oath, as prescribed by the Constitution: "I do solemnly swear that I will faithfully execute the Office of the

President of the United States, and will to the best of my ability, preserve, protect and defend the Constitution of the United States." Lincoln put the emphasis on the verb "defend" because he was faced with an armed insurrection. Later presidents, however, have zeroed in on the verb "execute"—as broad a verb, in this context, as any president on the loose could wish for. From this innocuous-seeming word have come the notions of inherent executive power and executive privilege, and that astonishing fact with which we have been obliged to live for half a century; the executive order.

Congress and Court can be bypassed by an executive order except on very odd occasions, such as Truman's unsuccessful seizure of the steel mills. When Wilson's request to arm merchant American ships was filibustered to death by the Senate in 1917, Wilson issued an executive order, arming the ships. Later, still on his own, Wilson sent troops to Russia to support the czar; concluded the armistice of 1918; and introduced Jim Crow to Washington's public places. In 1936 Franklin Roosevelt issued a secret executive order creating what was later to become, in World War II, the OSS, and then in peacetime [sic] the CIA. This vast enterprise has never even been moderately responsive to the Congress that obediently funds it. The CIA is now the strong secret arm of the president and no president is about to give it up.

For all practical purposes, the Second Republic is now at an end. The president is a dictator who can only be replaced either in the quadrennial election by a clone or through his own incompetency, like Richard Nixon, whose neurosis it was to shoot himself publicly and repeatedly in, as they say, the foot. Had Nixon not been helicoptered out of the White House, men in white would have taken him away. The fact that we may be living in an era of one-term presidents does not lessen, in any way, the formidable powers of the executive.

The true history of the executive order has yet to be written. As of December 31, 1975, the presidents had issued 11,893 executive orders. The Constitution makes no allowances for them. In fact, when an order wages war or spends money, it is unconstitutional. But precedents can always, torturously, be found for the president to "execute his office." In 1793, Washington proclaimed that the United States was neutral in the war between England and France, in contravention of the treaty of 1778 which obliged the United States to come to France's aid. In 1905 the Senate declined to approve a treaty that Theodore Roosevelt wanted to make with Santo Domingo. Ever brisk and pugnacious, TR made an agreement on his own; and a year later the Senate ratified it. In 1940 Franklin Roosevelt gave England fifty destroyers that were not his to give. But three years earlier, the Supreme Court had validated the principle of executive *agreement (U.S. v. Belmont);* as a result, the executive agreement and the executive order are now for the usurper president what judicial review has been for the usurper Court.

Law by presidential decree is an established fact. But, as Lundberg notes, it is odd that there has been no effective challenge by Congress to this usurpation of its powers by the executive. Lundberg quotes the late professor Edward S. Corwin of Princeton, a Constitutional scholar who found troubling the whole notion of government by decree: "It would be more accordant," wrote Corwin in *Court Over Constitution,* "with American ideas of government by law to require, before a purely executive agreement to be applied in the field of private rights, that it be supplemented by a sanctioning act of Congress. And that Congress, which can repeal any treaty as 'law of the land or authorization' can do the same to executive agreements would seem to be obvious." Obvious—but ignored by a Congress more concerned with the division of the contents of the pork barrel than with the defense of its own powers.

Between a president ruling by decrees, some secret and some not, and a Court making policy through its peculiar powers of judicial review, the Congress has ceased to be of much consequence. Although a number of efforts were made in the Congress during the 1950s to put the president back in his cage and to deflect the Court from its policymaking binges, nothing substantive was passed by a Congress which, according to Lundberg, "is no more anxious to restrict the president than it is to restrict the Supreme Court. Congress prefers to leave them both with a free hand, reserving the right at all times to blame them if such a tactic fits the mood of the electorate." When Congress rejected Carter's energy program, it was not blocking a president who might well have got around it with an executive order. Congress was simply ducking responsibility for a gasoline tax just as the president had ducked it by maliciously including them in the process. Actually, Congress does, from time to time, discipline presidents, but it tends to avoid collisions with the principle of the executive order when wielded by the lonely Oval One. So does the Supreme Court. Although the Court did stop President Truman from seizing the steel mills in the course of the Korean (by executive order) War, the Court did not challenge the principle of the executive order per se.

Since the main task of government is the collection of money through taxes and its distribution through appropriations, the blood of the Second Republic is the money-labor of a population which pays taxes to support an executive establishment of some ten million people if one includes the armed forces. This is quite a power base, as it includes the Pentagon and the CIA—forever at war, covertly or overtly, with monolithic communism. "Justice is the end of government," wrote Madison (*Federalist Paper* No. 52). "It is the end of civil society. It ever has been and ever will be pursued until it is obtained, or until liberty be lost in the pursuit." Time to start again the hard pursuit.

It was the wisdom of Julius Caesar and his heir Octavian to keep intact the ancient institutions of the Roman republic while changing entirely the actual system of government. The new dynasty reigned as traditional consuls, not as kings. They visited their peers in the Senate regularly—in J.C.'s case once too often. This respect for familiar forms should be borne in mind when We the People attend the second constitutional convention. President, Senate, House of Representatives must be kept as familiar entities, just as their actual functions must be entirely altered.

Thomas Jefferson thought that there should be a constitutional convention at least once a generation because "laws and institutions must go hand in hand with the progress of the human mind. As that becomes more developed, more enlightened, as new discoveries are made, new truths disclosed, and manners and opinions change with the change of circumstances, institutions must advance also, and keep pace with the times. We might as well require a man to wear still the coat which fitted him as a boy, as a civilized society to remain ever under the regimen of their barbarous ancestors."

Jefferson would be amazed to see how the boy's jacket of his day has now become the middle-aged man's straitjacket of ours. The amended Constitution of today is roomier than it was, and takes into account the national paunch; but there is little freedom to move the arms because, in Herder's words, "The State is happiness for a group" and no state has ever, willingly, spread that happiness beyond the group which controls it. The so-called "iron law of oligarchy," noted by James Madison, has always obtained in the United States.

Ten years ago Rexford Guy Tugwell, the old New Dealer, came up with Version XXXVII of a constitution that he had been working on for some years at the Center for the Study of Democratic Institutions at Santa Barbara. Tugwell promptly makes the mistake that Julius Caesar and family did not make. Tugwell changes names, adds new entities. Yet the old unwieldy tripartite system is not really challenged and the result is pretty conventional at heart because "I believe," said Tugwell, explaining his new arrangements, "in the two-party system." One wonders why.

The Framers wanted no political parties—or factions. It was their view that all right-minded men of property would think pretty much alike on matters pertaining to property. To an extent, this was—and is—true. Trilateral Commissions exist as shorthand symbols of this meeting of minds and purses. But men are hungry for political office. Lincoln felt that if the United States was ever destroyed it would be by the hordes of people who wanted to be officeholders and to live for nothing at government expense—a vice, he added dryly, "from which I myself am not free."

By 1800 there were two political parties, each controlled by a faction of the regnant oligarchy. Today, despite close to two centuries of insurrections and foreign wars, of depressions and the usurpations by this or that branch of government of powers not accorded, there are still two political parties, each controlled by a faction of the regnant oligarchy. The fact that the country is so much larger than it was makes for an appearance of variety. But the substance of the two-party system or non-system is unchanged. Those with large amounts of property control the parties which control the state which takes through taxes the people's money and gives a certain amount of it back in order to keep the populace docile while reserving a sizable part of tax revenue for the oligarchy's use in the form of "purchases" for the defense department, which is the unnumbered, as it were, bank account of the rulers.

As Walter Dean Burnham puts it, "The state is primarily in business to promote capital accumulation and to maintain social harmony and legitimacy." But expensive and pointless wars combined with an emphasis on the consumption of goods at the expense of capital creation has called into question the legitimacy of the oligarchy's government. Even the dullest consumer has got the point that no matter how he casts his vote for president or for Congress, his interests will never be represented because the oligarchy serves only itself. It should be noted that this monomania can lead to anomalies. In order to buy domestic tranquillity, Treasury money in the form of transfer-payments to the plebes now accounts for some 70 percent of the budget—which cannot, by law, be cut back.

In the 1976 presidential election, 45.6 percent of those qualified to vote did not vote. According to Burnham, of those who did vote, 48.5 percent were blue-collar and service workers. Of those who did not vote, 75 percent were blue-collar and service workers. The pattern is plain. Nearly 70 percent of the entire electorate are blue-collar and service workers. Since only 20 percent of this class are unionized, natural interest requires that many of these workers belong together in one party. But as 49 percent of the electorate didn't vote in 1980, the "two-party system" is more than ever meaningless and there is no chance of a labor party—or of any party other than that of the status quo.

The regnant minority is genuinely terrified of a new constitutional convention. They are happier with the way things are, with half the electorate permanently turned off and the other half mildly diverted by presidential elections in which, despite a semblance of activity, there is no serious choice. For the last two centuries the debate has been going on as to whether or not the people can be trusted to govern themselves. Like most debates, this one has been so formulated that significant alternative ideas are excluded at the start. "There are nations," said Herzen, "but not states." He saw the nation-state as, essentially, an evil—and so it has proved most of the time in most places during this epoch (now ending) of nation-states which can be said to have started, in its current irritable megalomaniacal form, with Bismarck in Germany and Lincoln in the United States.

James Madison's oligarchy, by its very nature, cannot and will not share power. We are often reminded that some 25 percent of the population are comprised of (in Lundberg's words) "the superannuated, the unskilled, the immature of all ages, the illiterate, the improvident propagators, the mentally below par or disordered" as well as "another 25 percent only somewhat better positioned and liable at any rum or whirligig of circumstances to find themselves in the lower category." As Herzen, in an unhappy mood, wrote, "Who that respects the truth would ask the opinion of the first man he meets? Suppose Columbus or Copernicus had put to the vote the existence of America or the movement of the earth?" Or as a successful movie executive, in a happy mood, once put it: "When the American public walks, its knuckles graze the ground."

The constant search for external enemies by the oligarchy is standard stuff. All dictators and ruling groups indulge in this sort of thing, reflecting Machiavelli's wisdom that the surest way to maintain one's power over the people is to keep them poor and on a wartime footing. We fought in Vietnam to contain China, which is now our Mao-less friend; today we must have a show-down with Russia, in order to . . . one has already forgotten the basis for the present quarrel. No. Arms race. That's it. They are outstripping us in warheads, or something. On and on the prop-aganda grinds its dismal whine. Second to none. Better to die in Afghanistan than Laguna. We must not lose the will. . . .

There are signs that the American people are beginning to tire of all of this. They are also angry at the way that their money is taken from them and wasted on armaments—although they have been sufficiently conned into thinking that armaments are as good as loafers on welfare and bureaucrats on the Treasury teat are bad. Even so, they believe that too much is being taken away from them; and that too little ever comes back.

Since Lundberg began his career as an economist, it is useful to quote him at length on how the oligarchy operates the economy—acting in strict accordance with the letter if not the spirit of the constitutions:

> The main decision that Congress and the President make that is of steady effect on the citizenry concerns appropriations—that is, how much is to be spent up to and beyond a half-trillion dollars and what for. The pro-ceeds are supposed to come from taxes but here, in

response to citizen sensitivity, the government tends to understate the cost. Because the government has taken to spending more than it takes in, the result is inflation—a steady rise in the prices of goods and services.

The difference between what it spends and what it takes in the government makes up by deviously operating the money printing machine, so that the quantity of money in circulation exceeds the quantity of goods and services. Prices therefore tend to rise and money and money-values held by citizens decline in purchasing value....

All that the government has been doing in these respects is strictly constitutional. For the Constitution empowers it, first, to lay taxes without limit (Article I, Section 8, Paragraph 1). It is empowered in the very next paragraph to borrow money on the credit of the United States—that is, the taxpayers—also without limit.... As to inflation, Paragraph 5 empowers the government, through Congress and the President, not only to coin money but to "regulate the value thereof." In other words, under the Constitution a dollar is worth whatever Congress and the President determine it to be by their fiscal decisions, and for nearly three decades officials, Republican and Democratic alike, have decreed that it be worth less ...

When Congress and president over-appropriate, the Treasury simply prints ... "short-term notes and bonds and sends these over to the Federal Reserve Bank, the nation's central bank. In receipt of these securities, the Federal Reserve simply credits the Treasury with a deposit for the total amount. The Treasury draws checks against these deposits. And these checks are new money. Or the Treasury may simply offer the securi-ties for sale in the open market, receiving there from the checks of buyers.

Since there is no legal way to control either President or Con-gress under the current system, it is inevitable that there would be a movement for radical reform. The National Taxpayers Union was organized to force the federal government to maintain a balanced budget. In order to accomplish this, it will be necessary to change the Constitution. So the National Tax-payers Union has called for a new constitutional convention. To date, thirty state legislatures have said yes to that call. When thirty-four state legislatures ask for a new convention, there will be one. As Professor Gerald Gunther of Stanford Law School recently wrote:

> The convention delegates would gather after popular elections—elections where the platforms and debates would be outside congressional control, where interest groups would seek to raise issues other than the budget, and where some successful candidates would no doubt respond to those pressures. Those convention delegates could claim to be legitimate representatives of the people. And they could make a plausible—and I believe correct—argument that a convention is entitled to set its own agenda. . . .*

* "Constitutional Roulette: The Dimensions of Risk" in *The Constitution and the Budget,* edited by W. S. Moore and Rudolph G. Penner (Amer-ican Enterprise Institute for Public Policy Research, Washington and London, 1980).

Those who fear that Milton Friedman's cheerful visage will be swiftly hewn from Dakota rock underestimate the passion of the majority not to be unemployed in a country where the gap between rich and poor is, after France, the greatest in the Western world. Since the welfare system is the price that the white majority pays in order to exclude the black minority from the general society, entirely new social arrangements will have to be made if that system is to be altered significantly.

Predictably, the oligarchs and their academic advisers view with alarm any radical change. The Bill of Rights will be torn to shreds, they tell us. Abortion will be forbidden by the Constitution while prayers will resonate in the classrooms of the Most Christian Republic. The oligarchs think that the people are both dangerous and stupid. Their point is moot. But we do know that the oligarchs are a good deal more dangerous to the polity than the people at large. Predictions that civil rights would have a rocky time at a new convention ignore the reality that the conglomeration of groups attending it will each have residual ethnic, ideological, religious, and local interests whose expression they will not want stifled. It is by no means clear that civil liberties would be submerged at a new convention; and there is no reason why the delegates should not decide that a Supreme Court of some sort should continue to act as protector of the Bill of Rights—a better protector, perhaps, than the court that recently separated a Mr. Snepp from his royalties.

The forms of the original republic should be retained. But the presidency should be severely limited in authority, and shorn of the executive order and the executive agreement. The House of Representatives should be made not only more representative but whoever can control a majority will be the actual chief of government, governing through a cabinet chosen from the House. This might render it possible for the United States to have, for the first time in two centuries, real political parties. Since the parliamentary system works reasonably well in the other industrially developed democracies, there is no reason why it should not work for us. Certainly our present system does not work, as the late election demonstrated.

Under a pure parliamentary system the Supreme Court must be entirely subservient to the law of the land, which is made by the House of Representatives; and judicial review by the Court must join the executive order on the junk-heap of history. But any parliamentary system that emerged from a new constitutional convention would inevitably be a patchwork affair in which a special niche could, and no doubt would, be made for a judicial body to protect and enforce the old Bill of Rights. The Senate should be kept as a home for wise men, much like England's House of life-Lords. One of the Senate's duties might be to study the laws of the House of Representatives with an eye to their constitutionality, not to mention rationality. There should be, at regular intervals, national referenda on important subjects. The Swiss federal system provides some interesting ideas; certainly their cantonal system might well be an answer to some of our vexing problems—particularly, the delicate matter of bilingualism.

The present Constitution will be two hundred years old in 1987—as good a date as any to finish the work of the second constitutional convention, which will make possible our Third Republic, and first—ah, the note of optimism!—civilization.

—*The New York Review of Books*
February, 1981

III

TEN

WE ARE THE PATRIOTS

I belong to a minority that is now one of the smallest in the country and, with every day, grows smaller. I am a veteran of World War II. And I can recall thinking,

when I got out of the Army in 1946, Well, that's that. We won. And those who come after us will never need do this again. Then came the two mad wars of imperial vanity—Korea and Vietnam. They were bitter for us, not to mention for the so-called enemy. Next we were enrolled in a perpetual war against what seemed to be the enemy-of-the-month club. This war kept major revenues going to military procurement and secret police, while withholding money from us, the taxpayers, with our petty concerns for life, liberty and the pursuit of happiness.

But no matter how corrupt our system became over the last century—and I lived through three-quarters of it—we still held on to the Constitution and, above all, to the Bill of Rights. No matter how bad things got, I never once believed that I would see a great part of the nation—of we the people, unconsulted and unrepresented in a matter of war and peace—demonstrating in such numbers against an arbitrary and secret government, preparing and conducting wars for us, or at least for an army recruited from the unemployed to fight in. Sensibly, they now leave much of the fighting to the uneducated, to the excluded.

During Vietnam Bush fled to the Texas Air National Guard. Cheney, when asked why he avoided service in Vietnam, replied, "I had other priorities." Well, so did 12 million of us sixty years ago. Priorities that 290,000 were never able to fulfill.

So who's to blame? Us? Them? Well, we can safely blame certain oil and gas hustlers who have effectively hijacked the government from presidency to Congress to, most ominously, the judiciary. How did they do it? Curiously, the means have always been there. It took the higher greed and other interests to make this coup d'état work.

It was Benjamin Franklin, of all people, who saw our future most clearly back in 1787, when, as a delegate to the Constitutional Convention at Philadelphia, he read for the first time the proposed Constitution. He was old; he was dying; he was not well enough to speak but he had prepared a text that a friend read. It is so dark a statement that most school history books omit his key words.

Franklin urged the convention to accept the Constitution despite what he took to be its great faults, because it might, he said, provide good government in the short term. "There is no form of government but what may be a blessing to the people if well administered, and I believe farther that this is likely to be well administered for a course of years, and can only end in Despotism, as other forms have done before it, when the people shall become so corrupted as to need despotic Government, being incapable of any other." Think of Enron, Merrill Lynch, etc., of chads and butterfly ballots, of Scalia's son arguing before his unrecused father at the Supreme Court while unrecused Thomas sits silently by, his wife already at work for the approaching Bush Administration. Think, finally, of the electoral college, a piece of dubious, antidemocratic machinery that Franklin doubtless saw as a source of deepest corruption and subsequent mischief for the Republic, as happened not only in 1876 but in 2000.

Franklin's prophecy came true in December 2000, when the Supreme Court bulldozed its way through the Constitution in order to select as its President the loser in the election of that year. Despotism is now securely in the saddle. The old Republic is a shadow of itself, and we now stand in the glare of a nuclear world empire with a government that sees as its true enemy "we the people," deprived of our electoral franchise. War is the usual aim of despots, and serial warfare is what we are going to get unless—with help from well-wishers in new old Europe and from ourselves, awake at last—we can persuade this peculiar administration that they are acting entirely on their vicious own, and against all our history.

The other night on CNN I brought the admirable Aaron Brown to a full stop, not, this time, with Franklin but with John Quincy Adams, who said in 1821, on the subject of our fighting to liberate Greece from Turkey, the United States "goes not abroad, in search of monsters to destroy." If the United States took up all foreign affairs, "she might become the dictatress of the world. She would no longer be the ruler of her own spirit," her own soul.

Should we be allowed in 2004 to hold a presidential election here in the homeland, I suspect we shall realize that the only regime change that need concern our regained spirit—or soul—is in Washington.

President Adams is long since dead. And we have now been in the empire business since 1898: We had promised to give the Filipinos their independence from Spain. Then we changed our mind, killing some 200,000 of them in the process of Americanizing them.

A few years ago there was a significant exchange between then-General Colin Powell and then-statesperson Madeleine Albright. Like so many civilians, she was eager to use our troops against our enemies: What's the point of having all this military and not using it? He said, They are not toy soldiers. But in the interest of fighting Communism for so long, we did spend trillions of dollars, until we are now in danger of sinking beneath the weight of so much weaponry.

Therefore, I suppose it was inevitable that, sooner or later, a new generation would get the bright idea, Why not stop fooling around with diplomacy and treaties and coalitions and just use our military power to give orders to the rest of the world? A year or two ago, a pair of neoconservatives put forward this exact notion. I responded—in print—that if we did so, we would have perpetual war for perpetual peace. Which is not good for business. Then the Cheney-Bush junta seized power. Although primarily interested in oil reserves, they liked the idea of playing soldiers too.

Last September Congress received from the Administration a document called the National Security Strategy of the United States. As the historian Joseph Stromberg observed, "It must be read to be believed." The doctrine preaches the desirability of the United States becoming-to use Adams's words-dictatress of the world. It also assumes that the President and his lieutenants are morally entitled to govern the planet. It declares that our "best defense is a good offense." The doctrine of pre-emption is next declared: "As a matter of common sense and self-defense, America will act against such emerging threats before they are fully formed." (Emphasis added.) Doubtless, General Ashcroft is now in Utah arresting every Mormon male before he can kidnap eight young girls for potential wives.

Article 1, Section 8 of the Constitution says that only Congress can declare war. But Congress surrendered that great power to the President in 1950 and has never taken it back.

As former Senator Alan Simpson said so cheerily on TV the other evening, "The Commander in Chief of the military will decide what the cause is. It won't be the American people." So in great matters we are not guided by law but by faith in the President, whose powerful Christian beliefs preach that "faith is the substance of things hoped for, the evidence of things not seen."

In response to things not seen, the USA Patriot Act was rushed through Congress and signed forty-five days after 9/11. We are expected to believe that its carefully crafted 342 pages were written in that short time. Actually, it reads like a continuation of Clinton's post-Oklahoma City antiterrorist act. The Patriot Act makes it possible for government agents to break into anyone's home when they are away, conduct a search and keep the citizen indefinitely from finding out that a warrant was issued. They can oblige librarians to tell them what books anyone has withdrawn. If the librarian refuses, he or she can be criminally charged. They can also collect your credit reports and other sensitive information without judicial approval or the citizen's consent.

Finally, all this unconstitutional activity need not have the slightest connection with terrorism. Early in February, the Justice Department leaked Patriot Act II, known as the Domestic Security Enhancement Act, dated January 9, 2003. A Congress that did not properly debate the first act will doubtless be steamrolled by this lawless expansion.

Some provisions: If an American citizen has been accused of supporting an organization labeled as terrorist by the government, he can be deprived of his citizenship even if he had no idea the organization had a link to terrorists. Provision in Act II is also made for more searches and wiretaps without warrant as well as secret arrests (Section 201). In case a citizen tries to fight back in order to retain the citizenship he or she was born with, those federal agents who conduct illegal surveillance with the blessing of high Administration officials are immune from legal action. A native-born American deprived of citizenship would, presumably, be deported, just as, today, a foreign-born person can be deported. Also, according to a recent ruling of a federal court, this new power of the Attorney General is not susceptible to judicial review. Since the American who has had his citizenship taken away cannot, of course, get a passport, the thoughtful devisers of Domestic Security Enhancement authorize the Attorney General to deport him "to any country or region regardless of whether the country or region has a government." Difficult cases with no possible place to go can be held indefinitely.

Where under Patriot Act I only foreigners were denied due process of law as well as subject to arbitrary deportation, Patriot Act II now includes American citizens in the same category, thus eliminating in one great erasure the Bill of Rights.

Our greatest historian, Charles Beard, wrote in 1939:

The destiny of Europe and Asia has not been committed, under God, to the keeping of the United States; and only conceit, dreams of grandeur, vain imaginings, lust for power, or a desire to escape from our domestic perils and obligations could possibly make us suppose that Providence has appointed us his chosen people for the pacification of the earth.

Those Americans who refuse to plunge blindly into the maelstrom of European and Asiatic politics are not defeatist or neurotic. They are giving evidence of sanity, not cowardice, of adult thinking as distinguished from infantilism. They intend to preserve and defend the Republic. America is not to be Rome or Britain. It is to be America.

—*The Nation*
June 2, 2003

ELEVEN

INTERIM REPORT: ELECTION 2004

It is often hard to explain to foreigners what an American presidential election is actually about. We cling to a two-party system in the same way that imperial Rome clung to the republican notion of two consuls as figureheads to mark off, if nothing else, the years they held office conjointly. They reigned ceremonially, but were not makers of the political weather. Our two official parties have, at times, actually dedicated themselves to various issues usually brought to their attention by a new president with a powerful popular mandate; hence, Franklin Roosevelt's New Deal, which gave, if nothing else, hope to a nation sunk in economic depression. Later, as he himself folksily put it, "Dr. New Deal has now been replaced with Dr. Win the War." Dr. Win the War, whether he calls himself Republican or Democrat, is still providing, in theory, employment and all sorts of other good things for a people who did not emerge from Depression until 1940 when Roosevelt began a military build up which, fifty-four years later, like a maddened sorcerer's apprentice, continues to churn out ever more expensive weapons built by an ever-shrinking workforce.

As American media is controlled by that corporate America which provides us with political candidates a well-informed electorate is not possible. What media does do well is personalize a series of Evil Enemies, who accumulate weapons of mass destruction (as we ourselves constantly do) to annihilate us in the night out of sheer meanness.

How then will a people, grown accustomed to being lied to about serious matters, behave during an actual presidential election in which billions of dollars have been raised to give us a generally false view of the state of our union? Right off, half the electorate will not vote for president. Those who do vote sometimes exhibit unanticipated trends. In all the recent polls (easily, alas, rigged by the way the questions are posed) the conquest of Iraq is more and more regarded as an expensive mistake. Despite the generally mendacious media, Americans, in general, seem to have got the point to the exercise. So during this primary season, rehearsal for the November election, is anything substantive happening politically? Quite a lot for those who know how to read the Pravda-like Murdochian media.

First, a spontaneous antiwar movement has been holding huge rallies (mostly unreported by the media). I spoke to 100,000 people on Hollywood Boulevard. The press pretended no one much was there that day, but a subversive picture editor ran a photo of the missing (in print) 100,000 antiwar protestors stretching from La Brea to Vine Street and filling up the boulevard. In the Democratic primaries, an obscure governor from Vermont tapped into the antiwar fervor that was building across the country. I am writing a few days before the first Democratic primary. Although Governor Dean had a strong lead for many weeks (if Murdoch

TV is to be trusted (!)), he is currently tied with Massachusetts Senator John Kerry and Representative Dick Gephardt, each running as an antiwar candidate although each voted to give Bush wartime powers leaving Dean the most immaculate of the anti-imperial candidates. Should Bush lose, a possibility not yet even whispered in TV land, it will be entirely due to one of the most ancient reflexes of the American electorate: a dislike of foreign wars in general and imperial wars in particular.

Ulysses S. Grant, a great man, a great general, a failed president: a recent graduate from West Point, he fought dutifully against Mexico (1846); later, he registered his hatred of that war: "To us it was an empire of incalculable value but it might have been obtained by other means. The Southern rebellion was largely the outgrowth of the Mexican war. Nations like individuals, are punished for their transgressions. We got our punishment in the most sanguinary and expensive war in modern times." A true American imperialist tells me that our greatest general and winner of the Civil War was sentimental because the war that we fought against Mexico gave us California and a half dozen other states, and wasn't the 1860 civil war really about the abolition of slavery? No, it was not, but our historians tend to be cut from the same material as the media. A lie repeated often enough becomes plain truth. Bush told us so often that Saddam Hussein was in league with Al Qaeda and the 9/11 attack on the U.S. that 60 percent of Americans still believe this to be true. Even so, the anti-imperial movement is growing throughout the land; and now gives unusual substance to the present election.

I am adding this postscript before the March 2 "super" primaries. Gen. Wesley Clark came and went. Gephardt went.

Dr. Dean went. Senator Edwards now challenges Kerry, the front-runner, and polls show each beating Bush in November.

So, if nothing else, the feckless Bush has not only given new meaning to the equally feckless Democratic party but he has, despite the best—that is, worst—efforts of the media, given new meaning to our corrupt political system as the United States is now starting to divide, consciously, between imperialists, eager for us to seize all of the world's oil resources, and the anti-imperialists who favor peace along with renewable sources of energy. The media is furious at this departure from their norm—baroque lies about the personalities of the contenders.

There is also, in many quarters, growing unease about the essential crookedness of our political system: Bush has raised close to $300 million, how? Perhaps the next election, should we survive this one, will have as its subject the necessity of a new Constitution, a dangerous but inevitable notion. That is when the most eloquent of the presidential candidates this year, Dennis Kucinich, should come into his own. He is already shaping up as the natural leader of an as-yet-unborn progressive alliance. Naturally, he is branded a leftist, the word used for any thoughtful conservative. But then, we have never had a left, or even much in the way of a coherent right. We tend to divide between up and down. The downs may now be on the rise.

INDEX

A

abortion, global gag rule and, 23

Acheson, Dean, 96

Adams, Abigail, 89

Adams, Brooks, 44–47, 49–50, 51

Adams, Henry, 46, 47–48, 50, 52

Adams, John, 90, 112, 131, 137

Adams, John Quincy, 47, 163

Affluent Society, The (Galbraith), 6

Afghanistan, U.S. strike on, 15–16

Aguinaldo, Emilio, 48, 49

AIDS relief plan, 22–23

air travel security, 19

Albright, Madeleine, 164

American empire
 critics of, 48–49
 decline of, 95–96, 119
 establishment of, 44–49, 118–19
 financial health of, 41–43
 Four Horsemen and, 45–51
 opposition to, 45
 planning of, 44–46

Anderson, John, 109, 121

anti-Semitism, 75–77

antiwar movement, 170–71

Armageddon
 evangelists and prediction of, 62–73
 Israel and, 64–66, 72–73
 nuclear war and, 66–78
 Reagan and, 69–73

arms race
 Armageddon and, 66–78

blueprint for, 97–98
 demonization of Soviets and, 52–54, 76, 83, 96–98, 108–9
 Gorbachev on, 73–75
 reasons behind, 42–43
 with Soviet Union, 52–54

Ashcroft, John, 91

atomic bombs, 29

B

Bakker, Jim, 64, 72

ballot fraud, 30–37

Bancroft, George, 45

Barron v. City of Baltimore, 139

Beard, Charles, 166–67

Bennett, William, 5, 92

Bill of Rights, 80–82, 89, 109–10, 136, 139–40, 143–44
 See also Constitution

Black Box Voting (Harris), 30

Black, Hugo, 110–11

Blummer, R. E., 23

Boston Tea Party, 123

British Empire, 41–42, 44

Brown, Aaron, 163

budget deficits, 16
 See also defense spending; federal budget

Burnham, Walter Dean, 151

Bush, George H. W.
 1988 campaign of, 35–36, 83–84
 invasion of Panama by, 84
 as president, 85

Bush, George W.